VISUAL QUICKSTART GUIDE

jQUERY

Steven Holzner

⊙ Peachpit Press

Visual QuickStart Guide

jQuery

Steven Holzner

Peachpit Press

1249 Eighth Street
Berkeley, CA 94710
510/524-2178
510/524-2221 (fax)

Find us on the Web at: www.peachpit.com
To report errors, please send a note to: errata@peachpit.com
Peachpit Press is a division of Pearson Education.

Editor: Judy Ziajka
Production Coordinator: Myrna Vladic
Compositor: Debbie Roberti
Proofreader: Liz Welch
Indexer: FireCrystal Communications
Cover Design: Peachpit Press

ISBN 13: 978-0-321-64749-8
ISBN 10: 0-321-64749-1

9 8 7 6 5 4 3 2 1

Printed and bound in the United States of America

Dedication

To Nancy, of course!

Acknowledgments

The book you hold in your hands is the product of many people's work. I would particularly like to thank Wendy Sharp and Judy Ziajka for their tireless efforts to make this book the best it can be and Ed Tittel for his careful technical review of the entire manuscript.

TABLE OF CONTENTS

Introduction   **ix**

Chapter 1:   Essential jQuery   1
About jQuery 2
Getting Started with jQuery 4
Selecting Page Elements by ID 6
Selecting a Set of Elements 8
Selecting Elements by Style 10
Running Code When a Page Is Ready 12
Selecting the First of a Set of Elements 14
Showing and Hiding Page Elements 16
Selecting One of a Set of Elements 18
Specifying Elements in a Hierarchy 20
Creating Visual Effects 22
Creating New HTML Elements 24

Chapter 2:   Selecting Elements the jQuery Way   27
Selector Examples 28
Meeting the Selectors 30
Selecting Direct Descendants 32
Selecting First and Last Children 34
Selecting the Nth Child 36
Selecting Elements with Specific Text 38
Selecting Elements by Attribute 40
Selecting Elements by Attribute Value 42
Checking the Type of Matched Elements 44
Selecting Elements by Position 46
Examining Checked Boxes and Radio Buttons . . . 48
Examining Elements That the User Selected 50

**Chapter 3:   Working with Elements
              the jQuery Way   53**
Function Examples 54
Looping over Elements in a Wrapped Set 56
Reading Attribute Values 58
Setting Attribute Values 60
Rewriting Elements' HTML 62

Rewriting Elements' Text. 64
Appending Content to Elements 66
Moving Page Elements. 68
Setting Element Width and Height 70
Wrapping Elements. 72
Inserting Elements. 74
Editing the value Attribute 76

Chapter 4:   Working with Events   79

Event Handling in JavaScript and jQuery 80
Binding an Event Handler to an Event 82
Binding Multiple Event Handlers. 84
Binding Event Handlers Using Shortcuts 86
Calling Event Handlers Only Once. 88
Unbinding Event Handlers 90
Using the Event Object 92
Getting Mouse Coordinates 93
Getting the Event Type. 95
Capturing Keystrokes 97
Capturing Hover Events. 99
Getting Event Targets 101

Chapter 5:   Visual Effects and Animation   103

jQuery Visual Effects Overview. 104
Showing and Hiding Page Elements 105
Showing and Hiding Elements
      with Duration 107
Toggling Element Visibility. 109
Toggling Element Visibility with Duration 111
Fading Elements Out 113
Fading Elements In 115
Sliding Elements Up 117
Sliding Elements Down 119
Toggling Sliding Operations 121
Partially Fading Elements 123
Creating Custom Animation 125

Chapter 6:   The jQuery Utility Functions   127

Examples of jQuery Utility Functions. 128
Looping over Object Members with $.each( ) . . . 129
Determining Browser Type with $.browser 131
Customizing HTML by Browser Type 133
Checking Browser Support for
      Specific Features 135
Creating Arrays 138
Searching an Array. 140

Filtering an Array 142
Eliminating Duplicate Elements from Arrays . . . 144
Checking Whether Data Is an Array 146
Mapping an Array. 148
Trimming Text. 150

Chapter 7:   Jumping into Ajax   153
About Ajax 154
Working with Ajax the Standard Way. 156
Using jQuery load( ) to Implement Ajax. 158
Using Callbacks with the load( ) Function 160
Passing Data to the Server 162
Passing Form Data to the Server 164
Using $.post( ) to Send Data to the Server 166
Using the jQuery $.get( ) Function 168
Using $.get( ) to Send Data to the Server 170

Chapter 8:   Using the Full Power of Ajax   173
About $.ajax( ) 174
Using $.ajax( ) to Download Text 176
Using $.ajax( ) to Post Data to the Server 178
Using $.ajax( ) to Get Data from the Server 180
Handling Ajax Errors. 182
Handling Ajax Timeouts 184
Handling XML. 186
Handling Ajax Events Globally 188

Chapter 9:   Using the jQuery Widgets   191
About Working with Widgets 192
Creating Accordion Widgets 193
Creating Datepicker Widgets. 196
Creating Dialog Widgets 199
Getting Data from Dialog Widgets. 202
Creating a Progressbar Widget 205
Creating a Slider Widget 208
Creating a Tab Widget 211
Adding Tabs to a Tabs Widget. 214

Index   217

INTRODUCTION

Welcome to the jQuery JavaScript library. jQuery is an open-source JavaScript kit for building Web applications so dynamic they jump off the page. Filled with special controls like calendars and tab folders, and special effects like wipes and fade-ins, jQuery is gaining popularity rapidly.

Perhaps most important, jQuery gives you excellent support for Ajax applications. Ajax is what allows you to access a Web server from a browser without a page refresh—that is, there's no blinking, no flicker when you download data behind the scenes with Ajax; you just download the data and then you can display it in a Web page using dynamic HTML techniques. No fuss no muss—and the end result is an application that looks more like a desktop application than a Web application.

With Ajax, the user can do something in a browser page, and the result of their action appears instantly, updated immediately in the browser window, without affecting the other contents of the window.

What's in This Book

jQuery is a JavaScript library full of tools ready to be used—which means that it's prewritten JavaScript, ready for you to put to work in your own Web pages. In this book, you get a guided tour of what makes jQuery so popular.

jQuery specializes in letting you select elements in a page, and it does that better than any other JavaScript library. You'll see how to create *wrapped sets* of elements in jQuery, so you can handle multiple elements at the same time. You'll also see how to manipulate wrapped sets of elements by changing their appearance, style, visibility, text, and even their HTML.

jQuery also comes packed with super-powerful utility functions, such as functions that let you determine which browser the user has and what its capabilities are. jQuery provides many utility functions and you'll get a look at the best ones in this book.

jQuery is known for its visual effects, which include slick-looking wipes, in which a sheet of color wipes over an element, and fades, in which an element and its background fade from view. In this book, you'll see what you can do with these kinds of effects.

You'll also learn about the jQuery widgets, which are popular controls that you can use in your Web pages: calendars, accordion controls (that let you open their pleats to see additional pages of content), sliders, tabs, and more. The jQuery widgets have a polished, professional look, and jQuery provides them for just about every purpose you can think of in Web pages.

Finally, of course, comes Ajax. This book includes two chapters on Ajax: one to show how to use basic skills, and one to get into truly advanced territory. When you finish this book, you'll be an expert on using Ajax with jQuery.

That's the game plan, then: to put jQuery to work and see it at its most impressive.

What You'll Need

You won't need much in this book besides a knowledge of HTML, some knowledge of JavaScript, and a Web browser.

Nearly all the examples in this book can be run from your hard disk, simply by opening them in a browser. You should be fairly familiar with basic JavaScript, however. If you're not, take a look at a good online tutorial before proceeding.

Some Ajax examples make use of PHP on the server, and those examples need to be placed on a Web server that supports the PHP online scripting language.

You won't need to know PHP to read this book, though—those examples are provided only to verify that you can send data to the Web server as well as download it using Ajax. If you don't have access to a PHP-enabled Web server, you can simply read along or skip those examples.

The code for the book is available at www.peacphit.com/jqueryvqsin a Zip file. When you unzip the Zip file, you'll get nine folders: one for each chapter.

✔ Tip

- It's better to run the code from the code files rather than typing it directly from the book. Some lines of code were too long for the width of the book and so had to be continued on the next line, and if you type those lines without reassembling them into a single line, you could confuse some browsers.

That's it then—we're ready to start. Let's begin by digging into the world of jQuery in Chapter 1.

ESSENTIAL JQUERY

You can argue that JavaScript was never really meant for prime time. Today's emphasis on rich Internet applications has thrust JavaScript into the forefront as more and more online applications—from Ajax to Zoho—rely on your browser to give you all the functionality of high-priced software.

JavaScript wasn't really ready for the Web 2.0 revolution. In fact, JavaScript support varies strongly by browser, making it a difficult platform to work with, and as a result, many JavaScript libraries have sprung up to smooth the way.

That's where jQuery comes in. It's one of the most popular JavaScript libraries around, and for good reason, as you'll find out in this book. Originally created by John Resig during his college days at the Rochester Institute of Technology, jQuery has come far and fast from its beginnings, and this chapter starts us off by showing you how to install jQuery and what jQuery can do.

About jQuery

A number of high-profile sites, such as the BBC, Digg, Intel, MSNBC, and Technorati, use jQuery. Let's see why by taking a look at what jQuery has to offer.

jQuery Is Cross-Browser

A huge issue facing JavaScript is that no two browsers handle JavaScript in the same way. The way you locate page elements so you can work with them in code varies from browser to browser in a way that makes programmers' hair stand on end. jQuery puts an end to that worry by giving you a common set of functions across all browsers.

jQuery Supports Ajax

Ajax (or Asynchronous JavaScript and XML) is what dragged JavaScript into the limelight recently, and what's made JavaScript libraries so popular. Ajax lets your browser access the server behind the scenes, without a page refresh, giving Internet applications the look and feel of desktop applications. jQuery provides one of the best Ajax interfaces around.

jQuery Selectors

Accessing page elements such as <p> and <h1> is tough in JavaScript, and it's made tougher by cross-browser issues. jQuery lets you address anything in a page with a much-needed selector language (based on Cascading Style Sheet, or CSS, selectors so it's easy to learn).

jQuery Handles Page Loads

When you work with the elements in a page, applying interactive styles and so on, you want access to those elements as soon as possible. But JavaScript usually goes in the <head> section of a page—which is loaded first—while the elements you access go in the <body> section. Although you can rely on the browser's onload event, which delays anything you do until the page is fully loaded, including all images, jQuery gives you access to page elements without waiting for all images to load.

jQuery Lets You Create HTML

As with most good JavaScript libraries, jQuery gives you control over what's in a page by letting you create and delete HTML elements at any time.

jQuery Supports Animation and Effects

jQuery also has a great selection of animation and visual effects (such as fadeouts), and you can impress your users with such effects as visual wipes and dissolves.

jQuery also supports easy dragging and dropping of elements in a page.

ABOUT JQUERY

Getting Started with jQuery

jQuery is a JavaScript library that comes in a JavaScript file with the extension .js. You can get jQuery from the official jQuery site, www.jquery.com, as shown in **Figure 1.1**.

Getting started with jQuery is as simple as downloading one file—the jQuery library— and connecting it to your Web pages with a `<script>` element.

In fact, it can even be easier than that—you don't even need to download jQuery at all to use it. We'll take a look at how that works after downloading jQuery the standard way.

To get and install jQuery:

1. Navigate your browser to http://www. jquery.com.

   This opens the main jQuery page you see in Figure 1.1.

2. Click the Download (jQuery) link at the lower right of the jQuery page, opening the download page (**Figure 1.2**).

   You're presented with a link to the latest version of the minimized jQuery library, which in Figure 1.2 is jquery-1.3.2.min.js.

   The minimized version of the library is the version that's meant to be read by browsers, not people. The line breaks are taken out along with other items to keep the library small for quick downloading when people take a look at your page.

   If you want the full, human-readable version of the jQuery library, click the Downloads tab you see in Figure 1.2. The full version of the library will have the same name, but without the ".min" in the name—for example, jquery-1.3.2.js.

   The full version looks the same to your browser as the minimized version. The only difference is that the full version is human-readable, nicely indented with spaces and line breaks.

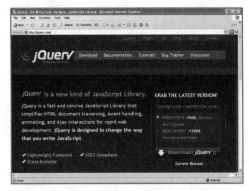

Figure 1.1 The official jQuery Web site, http://www. jquery.com/.

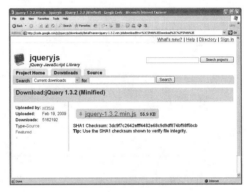

Figure 1.2 The jQuery library download page.

3. Click the name of the file you want to download (either the minimized or the full version).

Your browser displays a dialog box asking if you want to save or open the file.

4. Click the Save button and navigate to the folder in which you want to store the jQuery library on your computer.

5. Click Save.

6. When the download is complete, click the Close button.

7. Upload the jQuery library's .js file to the Web server that hosts the pages you want to use it with.

You can use the same method to upload the .js file as you use to upload Web pages—with an FTP application or browser.

The easiest way to install the jQuery library is to place it in the same folder on your Web server as the Web pages that will use it.

8. To give the JavaScript in an HTML page access to the jQuery library, insert this `<script>` element into the HTML page, in the `<head>` section, before any other `<script>` element where you want to use jQuery (substituting the name of the current version of the file for the one you see here):

```
<script type="text/javascript"
  src="jquery-1.3.2.js">
</script>
```

jQuery also maintains a version of its library online so you don't have to download it. You can use this `<script>` element instead to install the library in any Web page:

```
<script type="text/javascript"
→ src="http://code.jquery.com/jquery-
→ latest.js"></script>
```

Selecting Page Elements by ID

jQuery specializes in letting you pick out page elements so you can work on them. In this example, we'll see how to pick out a particular <p> element based on its ID attribute value.

When you use jQuery, you usually use a function named jquery() to gain access to the jQuery library. In fact, there's a shortcut: you can also call the function $(), and that's what we'll do.

To access an element with the ID "id", you call the function $(#id), which returns a set of all elements with that ID. Because IDs must be unique, that's only one element. To verify that we've selected a particular <p> element, we'll turn its background cyan when the user clicks a button with the jQuery toggleClass() function.

To select page elements by ID:

1. Use a text editor (such as Microsoft WordPad) to create your Web page. We'll use the example id.html from the code for the book here.

2. Enter the code to add the jQuery library to the page and give the third <p> element in the page the ID "third" (**Script 1.1**).

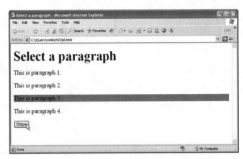

Figure 1.3 Selecting a page element and toggling its style.

Script 1.1 Giving the third <p> element an ID.

```html
<html>
  <head>
    <title>Select a paragraph</title>
    <script type="text/javascript"
      src="http://code.jquery.com/jquery-
        latest.js">
    </script>
    <script type="text/javascript">
    </script>
  </head>

  <body>
    <h1>Select a paragraph</h1>
    <div>
      <p>This is paragraph 1.</p>
      <p>This is paragraph 2.</p>
      <p id="third">This is paragraph
        3.</p>
      <p>This is paragraph 4.</p>
    </div>
    <form>
    </form>
  </body>
</html>
```

Script 1.2 Toggling the style of the third <p> element.

```
○ ○ ○                   Script
<html>
  <head>
    <title>Select a paragraph</title>
    <script type="text/javascript"
      src="http://code.jquery.com/jquery-
      latest.js">
    </script>
    <script type="text/javascript">
      function stripe() {
        $('#third')
        .toggleClass('striped');;
      }
    </script>
    <style>
      p.striped {
        background-color: cyan;
      }
    </style>
  </head>

  <body>
    <h1>Select a paragraph</h1>
    <div>
      <p>This is paragraph 1.</p>
      <p>This is paragraph 2.</p>
      <p id="third">This is paragraph
        3.</p>
      <p>This is paragraph 4.</p>
    </div>
    <form>
     <input type = "button"
      value="Stripe"
      onclick="stripe()"
     </input>
    </form>
  </body>
</html>
```

3. Add the code to select the third paragraph and toggle its style, giving it a cyan background when a button is clicked this way (**Script 1.2**).

4. Save the file.

5. Navigate to the file in your browser.

6. Click the button to give the third paragraph element a cyan background, as shown in **Figure 1.3** (in glorious black and white).

✔ Tip

- You can use the addClass() function instead of toggleClass() if you prefer.

Selecting a Set of Elements

When you pass a *selector* to the `jquery()` function—or the `$()` function, which is the same thing—you select a set of page elements.

Selectors are the topic of Chapter 2. They let you specify the page elements you want to work with. The previous task let you use the selector `#third` to select a `<p>` element with the ID `"third"`.

In this task, you'll select all the `<p>` elements in a page using the selector `"p"`, like this: `$("p")`. This selector returns a set of all `<p>` elements. We'll count the number of `<p>` elements in the set with the jQuery `size()` function and display that number in an alert box.

To select a set of page elements:

1. Use a text editor (such as Microsoft WordPad) to create your Web page. We'll use the example count.html from the code for the book here.

2. Enter the code to add the jQuery library to the page and add four `<p>` elements to the page (**Script 1.3**).

Script 1.3 Adding four `<p>` elements.

```
<html>
  <head>
    <title>Count paragraphs</title>
    <script type="text/javascript"
      src="http://code.jquery.com/jquery-
        latest.js">
    </script>
    <script type="text/javascript">
    </script>
  </head>

  <body>
  <h1>Count paragraphs</h1>
  <div>
  <p>This is paragraph 1.</p>
  <p>This is paragraph 2.</p>
  <p>This is paragraph 3.</p>
  <p>This is paragraph 4.</p>
  </div>
  </body>
</html>
```

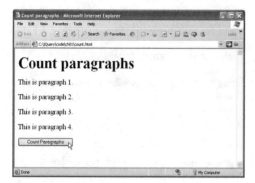

Figure 1.4 A set of <p> elements.

Script 1.4 Displaying the number of <p> elements.

```
<html>
  <head>
    <title>Count paragraphs</title>
    <script type="text/javascript"
      src="http://code.jquery.com/jquery-
        latest.js">
    </script>
    <script type="text/javascript">
     function count()
     {
       alert("There are " + $("p").size()
         + " paragraphs.");
     }
    </script>
  </head>

  <body>
  <h1>Count paragraphs</h1>
  <div>
  <p>This is paragraph 1.</p>
  <p>This is paragraph 2.</p>
  <p>This is paragraph 3.</p>
  <p>This is paragraph 4.</p>
  </div>
  <form>
   <input type = "button" value="Count
     Paragraphs"
   onclick="count()"
   </input>
  </form>
  </body>
</html>
```

3. Add the code to get a set of all <p> elements when the user clicks a button and to display the number of those elements (**Script 1.4**).

4. Save the file.

5. Navigate to the file in your browser. You should see the page that appears in **Figure 1.4**.

6. Click the button to have jQuery create a set of all <p> elements in the page and use the size() function to determine the size of the set.

You should see an alert dialog box with the message "There are 4 paragraphs."

7. Click OK to close the alert box.

✔ Tip

- This technique finds all the <p> elements in a page. They don't have to be adjacent or children of the same <div> element.

Selecting Elements by Style

You can also select page elements based on CSS *style*. For example, if you have a number of paragraphs and the second paragraph has been assigned the style class second, you can select that paragraph like this:

```
$('p.second')
```

If the paragraph elements are contained inside a <div> element, you can also indicate that (although it's not necessary), like this:

```
$('div p.second')
```

That is, you can create chains of selectors, as we're going to see in the next chapter. In this example, we'll let the user toggle the background of the second paragraph in the page by clicking a button.

To select elements based on style:

1. Use a text editor (such as Microsoft WordPad) to create your Web page. We'll use the example style.html from the code for the book here.

2. Enter the code to add the jQuery library and add four <p> elements to the page, giving the second paragraph the style "second" (**Script 1.5**).

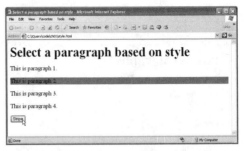

Figure 1.5 Selecting a page element based on style and toggling its style class.

Script 1.5 Giving a <p> element a style.

```
<html>
  <head>
    <title>Select a paragraph based on
      style</title>
    <script type="text/javascript"
      src="http://code.jquery.com/jquery-
      latest.js">
    </script>
    <style>
      p.second {
        font-weight: normal;
      }
    </style>
  </head>
  <body>
  <h1>Select a paragraph based on
    style</h1>
  <div>
  <p>This is paragraph 1.</p>
  <p class="second">This is paragraph
    2.</p>
  <p>This is paragraph 3.</p>
  <p>This is paragraph 4.</p>
  </div>
  </body>
</html>
```

Script 1.6 Selecting elements by style.

```
000                    Script
<html>
  <head>
    <title>Select a paragraph based on
      style</title>
    <script type="text/javascript"
      src="http://code.jquery.com/jquery-
        latest.js">
    </script>
    <script type="text/javascript">
      function stripe() {
        $('p.second')
          .toggleClass("striped");
      }
    </script>
    <style>
      p.second {
        font-weight: normal;
      }
      p.striped {
        background-color: cyan;
      }
    </style>
  </head>
  <body>
  <h1>Select a paragraph based on style
  </h1>
  <div>
  <p>This is paragraph 1.</p>
  <p class="second">This is paragraph
    2.</p>
  <p>This is paragraph 3.</p>
  <p>This is paragraph 4.</p>
  </div>
  <form>
   <input type = "button" value="Stripe"
   onclick="stripe()"
   </input>
  </form>
  </body>
</html>
```

3. Add the code to select the second paragraph and toggle a cyan background when the user clicks a button (**Script 1.6**).

4. Save the file.

5. Navigate to the file in your browser and click the button. You see the results shown in **Figure 1.5**.

Running Code When a Page Is Ready

jQuery lets you run your code when the page elements you want to work on have been loaded (better than the browser onload function, which is called only after all images have been loaded too). To run code when the page is ready, you use this syntax:

```
$(document).ready(function() {
    ...
});
```

There's a shorthand as well:

```
$(function() {
    ...
});
```

In this example, we'll add a style class to a <p> element to color its background cyan when the page loads. Note that this script wouldn't work unless you waited for the page to load, because the <p> element wouldn't be available to your code sooner (the code runs when the <head> section is loaded, not the <body> section).

To run code when a page is ready:

1. Use a text editor (such as Microsoft WordPad) to create your Web page. We'll use the example ready.html from the code for the book here.

2. Enter the code to add the jQuery library and add four <p> elements to the page, giving the second paragraph the style "second" (**Script 1.7**).

Script 1.7 Styling a <p> element.

```
<html>
  <head>
    <title>Running code when a page is
    ready</title>
    <script type="text/javascript"
      src="http://code.jquery.com/jquery-
      latest.js">
    </script>
    <style>
      p.second {
        font-weight: normal;
      }
    </style>
  </head>
  <body>
  <h1>Running code when a page is
    ready</h1>
  <div>
  <p>This is paragraph 1.</p>
  <p class="second">This is paragraph
    2.</p>
  <p>This is paragraph 3.</p>
  <p>This is paragraph 4.</p>
  </div>
  </body>
</html>
```

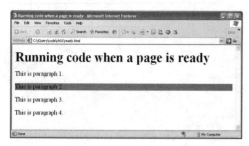

Figure 1.6 Running code when a page is ready.

Script 1.8 Selecting a <p> element.

```
<html>
  <head>
    <title>Running code when a page is
    ready</title>
    <script type="text/javascript"
      src="http://code.jquery.com/jquery-
      latest.js">
    </script>
    <script type="text/javascript">
      $(function() {
        $("p.second")
          .addClass("striped");
      });
    </script>
    <style>
      p.second {
        font-weight: normal;
      }
      p.striped {
        background-color: cyan;
      }
    </style>
  </head>
  <body>
  <h1>Running code when a page is
    ready</h1>
  <div>
  <p>This is paragraph 1.</p>
  <p class="second">This is paragraph
    2.</p>
  <p>This is paragraph 3.</p>
  <p>This is paragraph 4.</p>
  </div>
  </body>
</html>
```

3. Add the code to select the second paragraph and set its style to "second" when the page loads (**Script 1.8**).

4. Save the file.

5. Navigate to the file in your browser. You see the results shown in **Figure 1.6**.

Selecting the First of a Set of Elements

jQuery lets you select the first of a set of page elements using the positional selector named first.

As you'll see in Chapter 2, you use positional selectors as modifiers for other selectors, following a colon. For example, here's how to select the first <p> element in a page:

```
$('p:first')
```

You can change the style of the selected <p> element with the css() function, which accepts a CSS style and its new setting like this, where we're making the first paragraph italic:

```
$('p:first').css("font-style",
  "italic");
```

There's also a last selector that selects the last of a set of page elements:

```
$('p:last').css("font-style",
  "italic");
```

To select the first of a set of elements:

1. Use a text editor (such as Microsoft WordPad) to create your Web page. We'll use the example first.html from the code for the book here.

2. Enter the code to add the jQuery library and add four <p> elements to the page (**Script 1.9**).

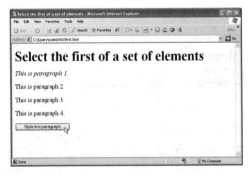

Figure 1.7 Accessing page elements by position in a page.

Script 1.9 Starting the sample page.

```
<html>
  <head>
    <title>Select the first of a set of
    elements
    </title>
    <script type="text/javascript"
      src="http://code.jquery.com/jquery-
        latest.js">
    </script>
  </head>

  <body>
  <h1>Select the first of a set of
      elements</h1>
  <div>
  <p>This is paragraph 1.</p>
  <p>This is paragraph 2.</p>
  <p>This is paragraph 3.</p>
  <p>This is paragraph 4.</p>
  </div>
  </body>
</html>
```

Script 1.10 Selecting the first paragraph.

```
                    Script
<html>
  <head>
    <title>Select the first of a set of
    elements
    </title>
    <script type="text/javascript"
      src="http://code.jquery.com/jquery-
        latest.js">
    </script>
    <script type="text/javascript">
      function setStyle()
      {
        $('p:first').css("font-style",
          "italic");
      }
    </script>
  </head>

  <body>
  <h1>Select the first of a set of
      elements</h1>
  <div>
  <p>This is paragraph 1.</p>
  <p>This is paragraph 2.</p>
  <p>This is paragraph 3.</p>
  <p>This is paragraph 4.</p>
  </div>
  <form>
   <input type = "button"
     value="Style first paragraph"
   onclick="setStyle()"
   </input>
  </form>
  </body>
</html>
```

3. Add the code to select the first paragraph and set its style to italics when the user clicks a button (**Script 1.10**).

4. Save the file.

5. Navigate to the file in your browser.

6. Click the button. You see the results shown in **Figure 1.7**, where the first paragraph has been selected and italicized.

Showing and Hiding Page Elements

jQuery lets you show and hide page elements easily.

You can hide a page element with the `hide()` function, which you use with a selector like this:

```
$('p:first').hide();
```

You can use the `show()` function to show page elements that have been hidden:

```
$('p:first').show();
```

To show or hide page elements:

1. Use a text editor (such as Microsoft WordPad) to create your Web page. We'll use the example hide.html from the code for the book here.

2. Enter the code to add the jQuery library and add four <p> elements to the page (**Script 1.11**).

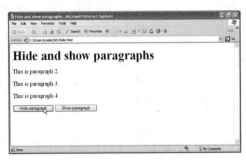

Figure 1.8 Hiding a paragraph.

Script 1.11 Creating a page with <p> elements.

```
<html>
  <head>
    <title>Hide and show
    paragraphs</title>
    <script type="text/javascript"
      src="http://code.jquery.com/jquery-
      latest.js">
    </script>
  </head>

  <body>
  <h1>Hide and show paragraphs</h1>
  <div>
  <p>This is paragraph 1.</p>
  <p>This is paragraph 2.</p>
  <p>This is paragraph 3.</p>
  <p>This is paragraph 4.</p>
  </div>
  </body>
</html>
```

Script 1.12 Hiding or showing elements.

```
<html>
  <head>
    <title>Hide and show
     paragraphs</title>
    <script type="text/javascript"
      src="http://code.jquery.com/jquery-
       latest.js">
    </script>
    <script type="text/javascript">
      function hide()
      {
        $('p:first').hide();
      }

      function show()
      {
        $('p:first').show();
      }
    </script>
  </head>

  <body>
  <h1>Hide and show paragraphs</h1>
  <div>
  <p>This is paragraph 1.</p>
  <p>This is paragraph 2.</p>
  <p>This is paragraph 3.</p>
  <p>This is paragraph 4.</p>
  </div>
  <form>
   <input type = "button" value="Hide
     paragraph"
   onclick="hide()"
   </input>
   <input type = "button" value="Show
      paragraph"
   onclick="show()"
   </input>
  </form>
  </body>
</html>
```

3. Add the code to select the first paragraph and hide or show it when the user clicks a button (**Script 1.12**).

4. Save the file.

5. Navigate to the file in your browser.

6. Click the Hide button. You see the results shown in **Figure 1.8**, where the first paragraph has been hidden.

7. To show the paragraph again, click the Show button.

✔ Tips

■ The show( ) and hide( ) functions are part of the visual effects that jQuery offers, and we'll be taking a more in-depth look at those visual effects throughout the book.

Selecting One of a Set of Elements

A jQuery expression like $('p') returns a set of all <p> elements in a page.

How does that set work? You can actually treat it like an array with an index value. For example, to select the first of a set of elements, you use an expression like this:

$('p')[0]

In this example, we'll rewrite the text in the <p> element, using the selected element's innerHTML property like this when the user clicks a button:

$('p')[0].innerHTML=
  "<i>Hello there!</i>";

To select one of a set of page elements:

1. Use a text editor (such as Microsoft WordPad) to create your Web page. We'll use the example index.html from the code for the book here.

2. Enter the code to add the jQuery library and add four <p> elements to the page (**Script 1.13**).

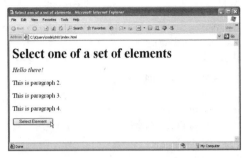

Figure 1.9 Selecting a paragraph by index value.

Script 1.13 Beginning the page.

```
<html>
  <head>
    <title>Select one of a set of
      elements
    </title>

    <script type="text/javascript"
      src="http://code.jquery.com/jquery-
        latest.js">
    </script>

  </head>

  <body>
  <h1>Select one of a set of
      elements</h1>
  <div>
    <p>This is paragraph 1.</p>
    <p>This is paragraph 2.</p>
    <p>This is paragraph 3.</p>
    <p>This is paragraph 4.</p>
  </div>

  </body>
</html>
```

Script 1.14 Rewriting the HTML of an element.

```
<html>
  <head>
    <title>Select one of a set of
      elements
    </title>

    <script type="text/javascript"
      src="http://code.jquery.com/jquery-
        latest.js">
    </script>

    <script type="text/javascript">
      function selectElement()
      {
        $('p')[0].innerHTML=
          "<i>Hello there!</i>";
      }
    </script>
  </head>

  <body>
  <h1>Select one of a set of
    elements</h1>
  <div>
    <p>This is paragraph 1.</p>
    <p>This is paragraph 2.</p>
    <p>This is paragraph 3.</p>
    <p>This is paragraph 4.</p>
  </div>

  <form>
   <input type = "button"
     value="Select Element"
   onclick="selectElement()"
   </input>
  </form>

  </body>
</html>
```

3. Add the code to select the first paragraph and rewrite its inner HTML to new text (**Script 1.14**).

4. Save the file.

5. Navigate to the file in your browser.

6. Click the Select Element button. You see the results shown in **Figure 1.9**, where the first paragraph has been rewritten.

Specifying Elements in a Hierarchy

jQuery is great at letting you select a set of elements. But what if you want to select one set in a page, but not another? Say you have some `<p>` elements in a `<div>` element that you want to select, but you don't want to select any `<p>` elements outside the `<div>` element.

One way of selecting the `<p>` elements you want is by specifying a selector hierarchy. For example, you can ask jQuery to select only those `<p>` elements that appear inside a `<div>` element, which itself appears in a `<body>` element, like this:

```
$('body div p')
```

This example lets you make the selection you want, and it also lets you change the style class of the selected elements when the user clicks a button, using this code:

```
$('body div
    p').toggleClass('striped');
```

To specify elements in a hierarchy:

1. Use a text editor (such as Microsoft WordPad) to create your Web page. We'll use the example hierarchy.html from the code for the book here.

2. Enter the code to add the jQuery library and add four `<p>` elements in a `<div>` element and one outside the `<div>` element (**Script 1.15**).

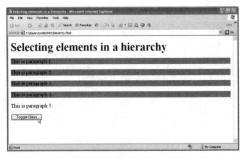

Figure 1.10 Selecting paragraphs.

Script 1.15 Adding `<p>` elements.

```
<html>
  <head>
    <title>Selecting elements in a
      hierarchy</title>
    <script type="text/javascript"
      src="http://code.jquery.com/jquery-
        latest.js">
    </script>
  </head>
  <body>
    <h1>Selecting elements in a
      hierarchy</h1>
    <div>
      <p>This is paragraph 1.</p>
      <p>This is paragraph 2.</p>
      <p>This is paragraph 3.</p>
      <p>This is paragraph 4.</p>
    </div>
    <p>This is paragraph 5.</p>
  </body>
</html>
```

Script 1.16 Selecting the first four paragraphs.

```
⊜ ⊜ ⊜                📄 Script
<html>
  <head>
    <title>Selecting elements in a
      hierarchy</title>
    <script type="text/javascript"
      src="http://code.jquery.com/jquery-
        latest.js">
    </script>
    <script type="text/javascript">
      function toggle()
      {
        $('body div
          p').toggleClass('striped');
      }
    </script>
    <style>
      p.striped {
        background-color: cyan;
      }
    </style>
  </head>
  <body>
    <h1>Selecting elements in a
      hierarchy</h1>
    <div>
      <p>This is paragraph 1.</p>
      <p>This is paragraph 2.</p>
      <p>This is paragraph 3.</p>
      <p>This is paragraph 4.</p>
    </div>
    <p>This is paragraph 5.</p>
    <form>
      <input type = "button"
        value="Toggle Class"
        onclick="toggle()"
      </input>
    </form>
  </body>
</html>
```

3. Add the code to select the first four paragraphs *only* and toggle their background to cyan (**Script 1.16**).

4. Save the file.

5. Navigate to the file in your browser.

6. Click the Toggle Class button.

You see the results shown in **Figure 1.10**, where only the first four paragraphs have been hidden.

Creating Visual Effects

jQuery also specializes in visual effects.

For example, to slide the first of a set of <p> elements (with the ID "first") up, you can execute this code:

```
$('#first').slideUp("slow");
```

To slide the element down visually, you can execute this code:

```
function slidedown()
```

The following example does both at the click of a button.

To slide page elements:

1. Use a text editor (such as Microsoft WordPad) to create your Web page. We'll use the example slide.html from the code for the book here.

2. Enter the code to add the jQuery library and add four <p> elements to the page, giving the first one the ID "first" (**Script 1.17**).

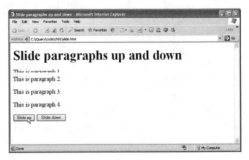

Figure 1.11 Hiding a paragraph.

Script 1.17 Giving a <p> element an ID.

```
<html>
  <head>
    <title>Slide paragraphs up and
      down</title>
    <script type="text/javascript"
      src="http://code.jquery.com/jquery-
        latest.js">
    </script>
  </head>

  <body>
    <h1>Slide paragraphs up and down</h1>
    <div>
      <p id="first">This is paragraph
        1.</p>
      <p>This is paragraph 2.</p>
      <p>This is paragraph 3.</p>
      <p>This is paragraph 4.</p>
    </div>
  </body>
</html>
```

Script 1.18 Sliding paragraphs around.

```
                    Script
<html>
  <head>
    <title>Slide paragraphs up and
      down</title>
    <script type="text/javascript"
      src="http://code.jquery.com/jquery-
        latest.js">
    </script>
    <script type="text/javascript">
      function slideup()
      {
        $('#first').slideUp("slow");
      }
      function slidedown()
      {
        $('#first').slideDown("slow");
      }
    </script>
  </head>

  <body>
    <h1>Slide paragraphs up and down</h1>
    <div>
      <p id="first">This is paragraph
        1.</p>
      <p>This is paragraph 2.</p>
      <p>This is paragraph 3.</p>
      <p>This is paragraph 4.</p>
    </div>
  <form>
   <input type = "button"
     value="Slide up"
     onclick="slideup()"
   </input>

   <input type = "button"
     value="Slide down"
     onclick="slidedown()"
   </input>
  </form>

  </body>
</html>
```

3. Add the code to slide the first paragraph up or down (hiding it or displaying it) at the click of a button (**Script 1.18**).

4. Save the file.

5. Navigate to the file in your browser.

6. Click the Slide Up button. You see the results shown in **Figure 1.11**, where the first paragraph is being hidden.

7. To show the paragraph again, click the Slide Down button.

Creating New HTML Elements

jQuery lets you create HTML elements and insert them into a page.

If you pass a text string that spells out a new HTML element to the jquery() or $() function (which are the same thing), jQuery will create that new element:

```
$("<p>I'm a new &lt;p&gt;
    element!</p>")
```

To actually get the new element into a page, you have to use a function like insertAfter(), passing a selector indicating the element that you want to insert the new element after.

This example creates new <p> elements and inserts them into a page following a <p> element with the ID "first", like this:

```
$("<p>I'm a new &lt;p&gt;
    element!</p>")
    .insertAfter("#first");
```

To create new elements:

1. Use a text editor (such as Microsoft WordPad) to create your Web page. We'll use the example create.html from the code for the book here.

2. Enter the code to add the jQuery library and add a <p> element with the ID "first" (**Script 1.19**).

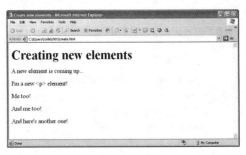

Figure 1.12 Creating new HTML.

Script 1.19 Adding a <p> element.

```
<html>
  <head>
    <title>Creating new elements</title>

    <script type="text/javascript"
      src="http://code.jquery.com/jquery-
        latest.js">
    </script>

  </head>

  <body>
    <h1>Creating new elements</h1>

    <p id="first">A new element is coming
      up...</p>

  </body>
</html>
```

Script 1.20 Creating new paragraphs.

```
<html>
  <head>
    <title>Creating new elements</title>

    <script type="text/javascript"
      src="http://code.jquery.com/jquery-
        latest.js">
    </script>

    <script type="text/javascript">
      $(function()
      {
        $("<p>And here's another
          one!</p>")
          .insertAfter("#first");

        $("<p>And me too!</p>")
          .insertAfter("#first");

        $("<p>Me too!</p>")
          .insertAfter("#first");

        $("<p>I'm a new &lt;p&gt;
          element!</p>")
          .insertAfter("#first");
      });
    </script>
  </head>

  <body>
    <h1>Creating new elements</h1>

    <p id="first">A new element is coming
      up...</p>

  </body>
</html>
```

3. Add the code to create four new <p> elements and insert them into the page (**Script 1.20**).

4. Save the file.

5. Navigate to the file in your browser. You see the results shown in **Figure 1.12**, where the new <p> elements have been inserted into the page.

✔ Tip

- Besides the insertAfter() function, there's also an insertBefore() function to insert HTML before another page element.

CREATING NEW HTML ELEMENTS

25

SELECTING ELEMENTS THE JQUERY WAY

One of jQuery's specialties is letting you select page elements so you can work on them.

You will often need to select page elements in online work. The selection capabilities of browsers are minimal and mostly involve the JavaScript `getElementByID` function, which requires you to add an ID value to any element you want to select (making selection of multiple items difficult, or at least time consuming).

CSS offers a much stronger set of tools for selecting page elements to set styles, and jQuery adopts many of the CSS selectors. Using the jQuery selectors lets you select page elements so you can work on them in JavaScript, not just with CSS styles.

You saw some basic selectors in the previous chapter, but jQuery has many more. We'll take a look at them here.

Selector Examples

Here are some examples of what selectors can do.

In the previous chapter, you saw that the selector

```
x
```

selects all elements of type x. The selector

```
x y
```

selects all elements of type y that have an element of type x as an ancestor.

What if you want to specify not only ancestors, but direct parents—that is, you want to match all y elements that are direct (first-generation) descendants of x elements? You can do that like this:

```
x > y
```

This code matches all y elements that have x elements as their direct parent.

How about finding the ninth <p> element in a page? You can do that with the eq selector:

```
eq(n)
```

Or suppose you want to match all even elements of a certain type (as when you want to stripe alternate rows of a table)? That's what this selector is for:

```
even
```

And because there's a selector for even elements, there's also one for odd elements:

```
odd
```

Do you want to match elements with attributes? Here's how to use a selector to match all elements that have a certain attribute:

```
[attribute]
```

What if you want to match only elements for which an attribute has a specific value? That code looks like this:

```
[attribute=value]
```

Or if you want to match the first child element of an element, that code looks like this:

```
first-child
```

There's a selector for the last child as well:

```
last-child
```

And what about the middle children? You can use this code:

```
nth-child(index)
```

You can also select on the type of a form element. For instance, you can use

```
radio
```

to select radio buttons.

And here's a very powerful selector: You can select on controls such as radio buttons that are presently selected in a Web page with this selector:

```
selected
```

Now let's get started exploring these selectors and more.

Meeting the Selectors

Table 2.1 lists some selectors. You can refer to this table as needed as you create your own jQuery pages.

Table 2.1

Some jQuery Selectors

SELECTOR	DOES THIS
#id	Selects a single element with the specified ID.
element	Selects all elements with the specified name.
.class	Selects all elements with the specified class.
*	Selects all elements.
selector1, selector2, selectorN	Selects the combined results of all the selectors.
ancestor descendant	Selects all descendant elements specified by descendant of elements specified by ancestor.
parent > child	Selects all direct child elements specified by child of elements specified by parent.
previous + next	Selects all elements specified by next that are next to elements specified by previous.
previous ~ siblings	Selects all sibling elements following the previous element that match the siblings selector.
:first	Selects the first selected element in the page.
:last	Selects the last selected element in the page.
:not(selector)	Removes all elements matching the specified selector.
:even	Selects even elements.
:odd	Selects odd elements.
:eq(index)	Selects a single element by its index number.
:gt(index)	Selects all elements with an index number greater than the specified one.
:lt(index)	Selects all elements with an index number less than the specified one.
:header	Selects all elements that are headers, such as h1, h2, and h3.
:animated	Selects all elements that are being animated.
:contains(text)	Selects elements that contain the specified text.
:empty	Selects all elements that have no children.
:has(selector)	Selects elements that contain at least one element that matches the specified selector.
:parent	Selects all elements that are parents.
:hidden	Selects all elements that are hidden.
:visible	Selects all elements that are visible.
[attribute]	Selects elements that have the specified attribute.
[attribute=value]	Selects elements that have the specified attribute with the specified value.

(table continues on next page)

Table 2.1 *continued*

Some jQuery Selectors	
SELECTOR	**DOES THIS**
[attribute!=value]	Selects elements that have the specified attribute but not the specified value.
[attribute^=value]	Selects elements that have the specified attribute and start with the specified value.
[attribute$=value]	Selects elements that have the specified attribute and end with the specified value.
[attribute*=value]	Selects elements that have the specified attribute and contain the specified value.
:nth-child(index/even/odd/equation	Selects elements that are the nth child or that are the parent's even or odd children.
:first-child	Selects all elements that are the first child of their parents.
:last-child	Selects all elements that are the last child of their parents.
:input	Selects all input elements.
:text	Selects all input elements of type text.
:radio	Selects all input elements of type radio.
:checkbox	Selects all input elements of type checkbox.
:enabled	Selects all elements that are enabled.
:disabled	Selects all elements that are disabled.
:checked	Selects all elements that are checked.
:selected	Selects all elements that are selected.

Selecting Direct Descendants

To select all <p> elements in a page that have <div> elements as ancestors, you can use this selector:

$('div p')

Note that this code selects all <p> elements that are descended from <div> elements. So this code matches this:

```
<div>
  <p>This is paragraph 1.</p>
</div>
```

And it also matches this:

```
<div>
   <span>
   <p>This is paragraph 1.</p>
   </span>
</div>
```

If you want to select only the first type of <p> elements—those with direct parent <div> elements—you can use this selector:

$('div > p')

That's what this example does.

To select direct descendants:

1. Use a text editor (such as Microsoft WordPad) to create your Web page. We'll use the example direct.html from the code for the book here.

2. Enter the code to add the jQuery library and some <p> elements in a <div> element to the page (the first <div> element is also inside a <span> element) as in **Script 2.1**.

Script 2.1 Adding <p> elements.

```
<html>
  <head>
    <title>Selecting direct
      descendants</title>
    <script type="text/javascript"
      src="http://code.jquery.com/jquery-
        latest.js">
    </script>
  </head>
  <body>
  <h1>Selecting direct descendants</h1>
  <div>
  <span>
  <p>This is paragraph 1.</p>
  </span>
  <p>This is paragraph 2.</p>
  <p>This is paragraph 3.</p>
  <p>This is paragraph 4.</p>
  </div>
  <p>This is paragraph 5.</p>
  </body>
</html>
```

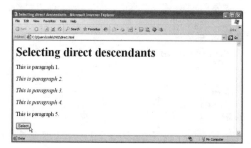

Figure 2.1 Italicizing matching <p> elements.

Script 2.2 Selecting only direct descendants.

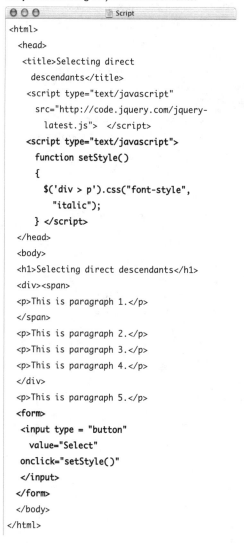

```
<html>
  <head>
    <title>Selecting direct
      descendants</title>
    <script type="text/javascript"
      src="http://code.jquery.com/jquery-
        latest.js">  </script>
    <script type="text/javascript">
      function setStyle()
      {
        $('div > p').css("font-style",
          "italic");
      } </script>
  </head>
  <body>
  <h1>Selecting direct descendants</h1>
  <div><span>
  <p>This is paragraph 1.</p>
  </span>
  <p>This is paragraph 2.</p>
  <p>This is paragraph 3.</p>
  <p>This is paragraph 4.</p>
  </div>
  <p>This is paragraph 5.</p>
  <form>
   <input type = "button"
     value="Select"
   onclick="setStyle()"
   </input>
  </form>
  </body>
</html>
```

3. Add the code to select only <p> elements with direct parent <div> elements and set their style to italics when a button is clicked (**Script 2.2**).

4. Save the file.

5. Navigate to the file in your browser.

6. Click the button to italicize the matching <p> elements (**Figure 2.1**).

Selecting First and Last Children

To select all <p> elements in a page, you can use this selector:

`$('p')`

To select all <p> elements that are the first children of their parent elements, you can use this selector:

`$('p:first')`

To select all <p> elements that are the last children of their parent elements, you can use this selector:

`$('p:last')`

To select first and last children:

1. Use a text editor (such as Microsoft WordPad) to create your Web page. We'll use the example firstlast.html from the code for the book here.

2. Enter the code to add the jQuery library and some <p> elements in a <div> element to the page (**Script 2.3**).

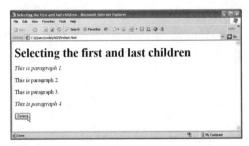

Figure 2.2 Italicizing the first and last <p> child elements.

Script 2.3 Starting a page with <p> elements.

```
<html>
  <head>
    <title>Selecting the first and last
      children
    </title>
    <script type="text/javascript"
      src="http://code.jquery.com/jquery-
        latest.js">
    </script>
  </head>
  <body>
  <h1>Selecting the first and last
    children</h1>
  <div>
  <p>This is paragraph 1.</p>
  <p>This is paragraph 2.</p>
  <p>This is paragraph 3.</p>
  <p>This is paragraph 4.</p>
  </div>
  </body>
</html>
```

Script 2.4 Selecting the first and last child elements.

```
<html>
 <head>
  <title>Selecting the first and last
   children
  </title>
  <script type="text/javascript"
   src="http://code.jquery.com/jquery-
    latest.js">
  </script>
  <script type="text/javascript">
   function setStyle()
   {
    $('p:first-child').css("font-
      style", "italic");
    $('p:last-child').css("font-
      style", "italic");
   }
  </script>
 </head>
 <body>
 <h1>Selecting the first and last
   children</h1>
 <div>
 <p>This is paragraph 1.</p>
 <p>This is paragraph 2.</p>
 <p>This is paragraph 3.</p>
 <p>This is paragraph 4.</p>
 </div>
 <form>
  <input type = "button"
    value="Select"
  onclick="setStyle()"
  </input>
 </form>
 </body>
</html>
```

3. Add the code to select only the first and last <p> child elements and italicize them when a button is clicked (**Script 2.4**).

4. Save the file.

5. Navigate to the file in your browser.

6. Click the button to italicize the first and last child <p> elements of the <div> element (**Figure 2.2**).

SELECTING FIRST AND LAST CHILDREN

Selecting the *N*th Child

jQuery allows you to select not just the first or last child element, but also the *n*th child element.

To select the *n*th child element, you use the nth-child selector

nth-child(n)

where *n* is the index number of the child.

For example, to match the third child element, you use this syntax:

nth-child(3)

To match the third child <p> element, you use this selector:

p:nth-child(3)

This example puts that selector to work.

To select the third child:

1. Use a text editor (such as Microsoft WordPad) to create your Web page. We'll use the example nth.html from the code for the book here.

2. Enter the code to add the jQuery library and some <p> elements in a <div> element to the page (**Script 2.5**).

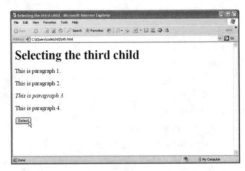

Figure 2.3 Selecting a child element by index number.

Script 2.5 Beginning the page.

```
<html>
  <head>
    <title>Selecting the third child
    </title>
    <script type="text/javascript"
      src="http://code.jquery.com/jquery-
        latest.js">
    </script>
  </head>

  <body>
  <h1>Selecting the third child</h1>
  <div>
  <p>This is paragraph 1.</p>
  <p>This is paragraph 2.</p>
  <p>This is paragraph 3.</p>
  <p>This is paragraph 4.</p>
  </div>
  </body>
</html>
```

Script 2.6 Selecting only the third child element.

```
<html>
  <head>
    <title>Selecting the third child
    </title>
    <script type="text/javascript"
      src="http://code.jquery.com/jquery-
        latest.js">
    </script>
    <script type="text/javascript">
      function setStyle()
      {
        $('p:nth-child(3)').css("font-
          style", "italic");
      }
    </script>
  </head>

  <body>
  <h1>Selecting the third child</h1>
  <div>
  <p>This is paragraph 1.</p>
  <p>This is paragraph 2.</p>
  <p>This is paragraph 3.</p>
  <p>This is paragraph 4.</p>
  </div>
  <form>
   <input type = "button"
     value="Select"
   onclick="setStyle()"
   </input>
  </form>
  </body>
</html>
```

3. Add the code to select only the third
<p> child element and italicize it when
a button is clicked (**Script 2.6**).

4. Save the file.

5. Navigate to the file in your browser.

6. Click the button to italicize the third
child <p> element of the <div> element
(**Figure 2.3**).

✔ Tip

■ You can also select all even-numbered
children by passing "even" to nth-
child( ) or all odd-numbered children
by passing "odd" to nth-child( ).

Selecting Elements with Specific Text

jQuery lets you further refine your search for particular elements by requesting elements containing specific text. You can't easily perform this same task using the same JavaScript in multiple browsers, so jQuery saves you a lot of time here.

To select elements containing particular text, use the selector

```
contains(text)
```

where text is the text you're searching for.

For example, to match the <p> element that contains the text "3" (as in "This is paragraph 3"), use this selector:

```
p:contains("3))
```

This example put that selector to work.

To select elements with specific text:

1. Use a text editor (such as Microsoft WordPad) to create your Web page. We'll use the example text.html from the code for the book here.

2. Enter the code to add the jQuery library and some <p> elements in a <div> element to the page (**Script 2.7**).

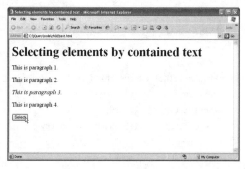

Figure 2.4 Selecting a child element with specific text.

Script 2.7 Adding some <p> elements.

```
<html>
  <head>
    <title>Selecting elements by
      contained text
    </title>
    <script type="text/javascript"
      src="http://code.jquery.com/jquery-
        latest.js">
    </script>
  </head>

  <body>
  <h1>Selecting elements by contained
      text</h1>
  <div>
  <p>This is paragraph 1.</p>
  <p>This is paragraph 2.</p>
  <p>This is paragraph 3.</p>
  <p>This is paragraph 4.</p>
  </div>
  </body>
</html>
```

Script 2.8 Searching for text in an element.

```
<html>
  <head>
    <title>Selecting elements by
      contained text
    </title>
    <script type="text/javascript"
      src="http://code.jquery.com/jquery-
        latest.js">
    </script>
    <script type="text/javascript">
      function setStyle()
      {
        $('p:contains("3")').css("font-
          style", "italic");
      }
    </script>
  </head>

  <body>
  <h1>Selecting elements by contained
      text</h1>
  <div>
  <p>This is paragraph 1.</p>
  <p>This is paragraph 2.</p>
  <p>This is paragraph 3.</p>
  <p>This is paragraph 4.</p>
  </div>
  <form>
   <input type = "button"
     value="Select"
   onclick="setStyle()"
   </input>
  </form>
  </body>
</html>
```

3. Add the code to select the third <p> child element and italicize it by searching for the text "3" when a button is clicked (**Script 2.8**).

4. Save the file.

5. Navigate to the file in your browser.

6. Click the button to italicize the third child <p> element of the <div> element (**Figure 2.4**).

Selecting Elements by Attribute

jQuery lets you select page elements based on their attributes, which enables you to differentiate elements of the same type.

To select elements based on their attributes, use the selector

`[attribute]`

where `attribute` is the attribute you're searching for.

For example, to match the `<p>` elements that have a `language` attribute, use this selector:

`$('p[language]')`

This example puts that selector to work.

To select elements by attribute:

1. Use a text editor (such as Microsoft WordPad) to create your Web page. We'll use the example attribute.html from the code for the book here.

2. Enter the code to add the jQuery library and some `<p>` elements, one with a `language` attribute, in a `<div>` element to the page (**Script 2.9**).

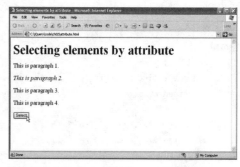

Figure 2.5 Selecting a child element by attribute.

Script 2.9 Giving a `<p>` element a language attribute.

```
<html>
  <head>
    <title>Selecting elements by
      attribute<title>
    <script type="text/javascript"
      src="http://code.jquery.com/jquery-
        latest.js">
    </script>
  </head>

  <body>
  <h1>Selecting elements by
    attribute</h1>
  <div>
  <p>This is paragraph 1.</p>
  <p language="English">This is paragraph
    2.</p>
  <p>This is paragraph 3.</p>
  <p>This is paragraph 4.</p>
  </div>
  </body>
</html>
```

Script 2.10 Accessing the language attribute.

```
○ ○ ○                    📄 Script
<html>
  <head>
    <title>Selecting elements by
      attribute
    </title>
    <script type="text/javascript"
      src="http://code.jquery.com/jquery-
        latest.js">
    </script>
    <script type="text/javascript">
      function setStyle()
      {
        $('p[language]').css(
          "font-style", "italic");
      }
    </script>
  </head>

  <body>
  <h1>Selecting elements by
      attribute</h1>
  <div>
  <p>This is paragraph 1.</p>
  <p language="English">This is paragraph
    2.</p>
  <p>This is paragraph 3.</p>
  <p>This is paragraph 4.</p>
  </div>
  <form>
   <input type = "button"
     value="Select"
   onclick="setStyle()"
   </input>
  </form>
  </body>
</html>
```

3. Add the code to select the <p> element with the language attribute and italicize it when a button is clicked (**Script 2.10**).

4. Save the file.

5. Navigate to the file in your browser.

6. Click the button to italicize the <p> element with the language attribute (**Figure 2.5**).

Selecting Elements by Attribute Value

jQuery lets you select page elements based not only on whether the element has a certain attribute, but also on the attribute's value.

To select elements based on their attribute values, use the selector

[attribute='value']

where attribute is the attribute you're searching for, and value is the value you want the attribute to hold.

For example, to match <p> elements with the language attribute set to 'German', use this selector:

$('p[language='German']')

This example puts that selector to work.

To select elements by attribute value:

1. Use a text editor (such as Microsoft WordPad) to create your Web page. We'll use the example attributevalue.html from the code for the book here.

2. Enter the code to add the jQuery library and some <p> elements, one with a language attribute set to "German", in a <div> element to the page (**Script 2.11**).

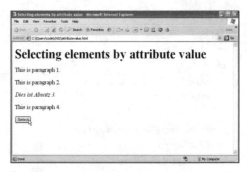

Figure 2.6 Selecting an element by attribute value.A

Script 2.11 Setting the language attribute.

```
<html>
  <head>
    <title>Selecting elements by
      attribute value
    </title>
    <script type="text/javascript"
      src="http://code.jquery.com/jquery-
        latest.js">
    </script>
  </head>
  <body>
  <h1>Selecting elements by attribute
    value</h1>
  <div>
  <p>This is paragraph 1.</p>
  <p language="English">This is paragraph
    2.</p>
  <p language="German">Dies ist Absatz
    3.</p>
  <p>This is paragraph 4.</p>
  </div>
  </body>
</html>
```

Script 2.12 Checking an attribute value.

```
○ ○ ○              📄 Script
<html>
  <head>
    <title>Selecting elements by
      attribute value </title>
    <script type="text/javascript"
      src="http://code.jquery.com/jquery-
        latest.js">
    </script>
    <script type="text/javascript">
      function setStyle()
      {
        $('p[language="German"]')
          .css("font-style",
          "italic");
      }
    </script>
  </head>
<body>
<h1>Selecting elements by attribute
  value</h1>
<div>
<p>This is paragraph 1.</p>
<p language="English">This is paragraph
  2.</p>
<p language="German">Dies ist Absatz
  3.</p>
<p>This is paragraph 4.</p>
</div>
<form>
 <input type = "button"
    value="Select"
 onclick="setStyle()"
 </input>
</form>
 </body>
</html>
```

3. Add the code to select the <p> element with the language attribute set to "German" and italicize it when a button is clicked (**Script 2.12**).

4. Save the file.

5. Navigate to the file in your browser.

6. Click the button to italicize the <p> element with the language attribute set to "German" (**Figure 2.6**).

Checking the Type of Matched Elements

jQuery lets you check the type of matched elements with the is() function. This function can be useful when you've matched a whole set of elements, but you want to work with only one particular type of matched elements: for example, <p> elements.

To use the is() function, you enter code like this:

```
$('#p1').is('p')
```

This selector returns true if the element with ID p1 is a <p> element.

This example puts that selector to work.

To determine the type of a matched element:

1. Use a text editor (such as Microsoft WordPad) to create your Web page. We'll use the example is.html from the code for the book here.

2. Enter the code to add the jQuery library and some <p> elements with various ID values to the page (**Script 2.13**).

Script 2.13 Adding ID values.

```
<html>
  <head>
    <title>Checking the types of matches
    </title>
    <script type="text/javascript"
      src="http://code.jquery.com/jquery-
        latest.js">
    </script>
  </head>

  <body>
  <h1>Checking the types of matches</h1>
  <div>
  <p id="p1">This is paragraph 1.</p>
  <p id="p2">This is paragraph 2.</p>
  <p id="p3">This is paragraph 3.</p>
  <p id="p4">This is paragraph 4.</p>
  </div>
  </body>
</html>
```

Figure 2.7 Checking the type of a particular element.

Script 2.14 Checking on <p> elements.

```
<html>
  <head>
    <title>Checking the types of matches
    </title>
    <script type="text/javascript"
      src="http://code.jquery.com/jquery-
        latest.js">
    </script>
    <script type="text/javascript">
      function checkType()
      {
        if($('#p1').is('p')){
          alert("The element with ID p1
            is a <p> element");
        }
      }
    </script>
  </head>

  <body>
  <h1>Checking the types of matches</h1>
  <div>
  <p id="p1">This is paragraph 1.</p>
  <p id="p2">This is paragraph 2.</p>
  <p id="p3">This is paragraph 3.</p>
  <p id="p4">This is paragraph 4.</p>
  </div>
  <form>
   <input type = "button"
     value="Select"
   onclick="checkType()"
   </input>
  </form>
  </body>
</html>
```

3. Add the code to select the element with the ID p1 and display an alert box if it is a <p> element (**Script 2.14**).

4. Save the file.

5. Navigate to the file in your browser.

6. Click the button to confirm that the element with the ID p1 is a <p> element (**Figure 2.7**).

CHECKING THE TYPE OF MATCHED ELEMENTS

Selecting Elements by Position

jQuery lets you select page elements by their position in a page.

For example, you can select all <p> elements in a page with this selector:

```
$("p")
```

If you want only the third <p> element, however, you can select it like this:

```
$("p:eq(2)")
```

Note that the page index number is zero based (that is, page index numbers begin at zero), so the third <p> element corresponds to index 2.

This example puts this selector to work.

To select elements by position:

1. Use a text editor (such as Microsoft WordPad) to create your Web page. We'll use the example eq.html from the code for the book here.

2. Enter the code to add the jQuery library and some <p> elements in a <div> element to the page (**Script 2.15**).

Script 2.15 Adding several <p> elements.

```
<html>
  <head>
    <title>Selecting one of a set
    </title>
    <script type="text/javascript"
      src="http://code.jquery.com/jquery-
        latest.js">
    </script>
  </head>

  <body>
  <h1>Selecting one of a set</h1>
  <div>
  <p id="p1">This is paragraph 1.</p>
  <p id="p2">This is paragraph 2.</p>
  <p id="p3">This is paragraph 3.</p>
  <p id="p4">This is paragraph 4.</p>
  </div>
  </body>
</html>
```

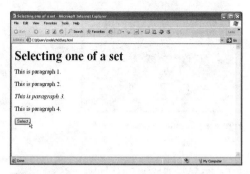

Figure 2.8 Selecting an element by position on the page.

Script 2.16 Selecting an element by index value.

```
<html>
  <head>
    <title>Selecting one of a set
    </title>
    <script type="text/javascript"
      src="http://code.jquery.com/jquery-
        latest.js">
    </script>
    <script type="text/javascript">
      function setStyle()
      {
        $("p:eq(2)").css("font-style",
          "italic");
      }
    </script>
  </head>

  <body>
  <h1>Selecting one of a set</h1>
  <div>
  <p id="p1">This is paragraph 1.</p>
  <p id="p2">This is paragraph 2.</p>
  <p id="p3">This is paragraph 3.</p>
  <p id="p4">This is paragraph 4.</p>
  </div>
  <form>
   <input type = "button"
     value="Select"
   onclick="setStyle()"
   </input>
  </form>
  </body>
</html>
```

3. Add the code to select the `<p>` element with the index value 2 and italicize it when the user clicks a button (**Script 2.16**).

4. Save the file.

5. Navigate to the file in your browser.

6. Click the button to italicize the third `<p>` element (**Figure 2.8**).

✔ Tip

■ In addition to using `eq` to match a particular page position, you can use `gt` to match all elements after a specific page position or `lt` to match all elements before a specific page position.

Examining Checked Boxes and Radio Buttons

One of the most powerful selectors is checked, which lets you select checked check boxes and selected radio buttons.

We'll put checked to work by counting the number of check boxes the user has checked.

To examine checked check boxes and radio buttons:

1. Use a text editor (such as Microsoft WordPad) to create your Web page. We'll use the example checked.html from the code for the book here.

2. Enter the code to add the jQuery library and some check boxes to the page (**Script 2.17**).

Figure 2.9 Counting checked check boxes.

Script 2.17 Adding some check boxes.

```
<html>
  <head>
    <title>Counting checked checkboxes
    </title>
    <script type="text/javascript"
      src="http://code.jquery.com/jquery-
        latest.js">
    </script>
  </head>

  <body>
  <h1>Counting checked checkboxes</h1>
  <form>
   <input type = "checkbox">
   Check 1
   </input>
   <input type = "checkbox">
   Check 2
   </input>
   <input type = "checkbox">
   Check 3
   </input>
   <input type = "checkbox">
   Check 4
   </input>
  </form>
  </body>
</html>
```

Script 2.18 Counting checked check boxes.

```
<html>
  <head>
    <title>Counting checked checkboxes
    </title>
    <script type="text/javascript"
      src="http://code.jquery.com/jquery-
        latest.js">
    </script>
    <script type="text/javascript">
      function count()
      {
        alert("You checked " +
        $("input:checked").length +
        " items.");
      }
    </script>
  </head>

  <body>
  <h1>Counting checked checkboxes</h1>
  <form>
   <input type = "checkbox">
   Check 1
   </input>
   <input type = "checkbox">
   Check 2
   </input>
   <input type = "checkbox">
   Check 3
   </input>
   <input type = "checkbox">
   Check 4
   </input>
   <br>
   <input type = "button"
     value="Count"
   onclick="count()"
   </input>
  </form>
  </body>
</html>
```

3. Add the code to count the number of checked check boxes when the user clicks a button (**Script 2.18**).

4. Save the file.

5. Navigate to the file in your browser.

6. Check some check boxes and click the button to count how many are checked (**Figure 2.9**).

EXAMINING CHECKED BOXES AND RADIO BUTTONS

Examining Elements That the User Selected

jQuery lets you select elements that have been selected by the user. For example, you might have a list box (that is, a <select> control) in which the user has selected several items. You can match those selected items with the selected selector, like this:

```
$("select option:selected")
```

This example puts this selector to work by counting the number of items the user has selected in a list box.

To select user-selected elements:

1. Use a text editor (such as Microsoft WordPad) to create your Web page. We'll use the example selected.html from the code for the book here.

2. Enter the code to add the jQuery library and a multiple-selection list box to the page (**Script 2.19**).

Script 2.19 Adding a multiple-select list box.

```
○ ○ ○              Script
<html>
  <head>
    <title>Counting selected items
    </title>
    <script type="text/javascript"
      src="http://code.jquery.com/jquery-
        latest.js">
    </script>
  </head>

  <body>
  <h1>Counting selected items</h1>
  <form>
    <select size="4" multiple="true">
      <option>Item 1</option>
      <option>Item 2</option>
      <option>Item 3</option>
      <option>Item 4</option>
    </select>
  </form>
  </body>
</html>
```

Figure 2.10 Counting the number of user-selected items.

3. Add the code to count the number of items in the list box that the user has selected (**Script 2.20**).

4. Save the file.

5. Navigate to the file in your browser.

6. Click the button to count the number of items selected by the user (**Figure 2.10**).

Script 2.20 Counting the number of selected items in a list box.

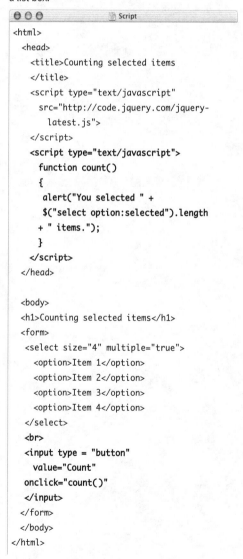

```
<html>
  <head>
    <title>Counting selected items
    </title>
    <script type="text/javascript"
      src="http://code.jquery.com/jquery-
        latest.js">
    </script>
    <script type="text/javascript">
      function count()
      {
        alert("You selected " +
        $("select option:selected").length
        + " items.");
      }
    </script>
  </head>

  <body>
  <h1>Counting selected items</h1>
  <form>
   <select size="4" multiple="true">
     <option>Item 1</option>
     <option>Item 2</option>
     <option>Item 3</option>
     <option>Item 4</option>
   </select>
   <br>
   <input type = "button"
     value="Count"
   onclick="count()"
   </input>
  </form>
  </body>
</html>
```

WORKING WITH ELEMENTS THE JQUERY WAY

In this chapter, we'll take a guided tour of jQuery's features for working with the elements and attributes in a page—all designed to let you access and manipulate page elements easily.

For instance, jQuery lets you access elements to change their HTML and text, set and read element attributes, and add new elements to a page and remove others.

All these manipulations are possible with jQuery functions (they're actually jQuery methods, but the distinction between functions and methods is sometimes blurred in jQuery, so we'll refer to them as functions).

Function Examples

This chapter explores a range of jQuery functions that will help you work with elements.

For example, you can use the each( ) function to apply a function to each of a set of elements. Although jQuery automatically applies a function such as css( ) to all members of an element set, you may want to do more than apply an existing jQuery function to all members of an element set: for example, you may want to create a custom alt attribute for all <img> elements in a page. To do this, you can create your own function and then use the each( ) function inside that function to loop over all members of the set.

jQuery also lets you directly access the HTML and text of page elements, with the html( ) and text( ) functions. Browsers typically support some or all of the innerHTML( ), outerHTML( ), innerText( ), and outerText( ) functions, but support varies by browser. By using html( ) and text( ), you'll automatically be compliant with all browsers.

You'll also see how to change the structure of a page with functions such as append( ) and insertAfter( ). Using functions like these, you can alter the structure of a page, moving HTML elements around and adding others right before the user's eyes.

Other jQuery functions we'll explore here include wrap( ), which lets you wrap elements inside another (such as wrapping <p> elements inside a <div> element) and clone( ), which lets you clone elements.

jQuery gives you the power and convenience that various browsers either leave out or support in different ways. For example, the jQuery `width()` and `height()` functions return the width and height of page elements—which you would think would be simple to find on your own. But if elements don't have explicit width and height attributes, finding these values is no easy matter, and you're often left trying to read such elements' width and height CSS style properties. However, elements have explicit width and height properties only if you've first set them explicitly yourself. The jQuery `width()` and `height()` functions have no such restrictions—they always work, whether or not you've set an element's CSS width and height style properties.

jQuery also has a number of functions that let you work with form elements, such as text fields. For example, the `val()` function returns the value of a form element. You can also use jQuery to set the value of a form element.

We'll explore other jQuery functions in this chapter as well.

FUNCTION EXAMPLES

Looping over Elements in a Wrapped Set

When you create a set of elements with the jQuery $( ) function and then apply a function such as css( ) to the set, jQuery applies the css( ) function to all members of the set automatically.

However, sometimes you may want to apply a custom function—one that you write yourself—to the members of a set. For example, you may want to add a custom alt attribute to all <img> elements in a set.

You can start with this code, which lets you loop all <img> elements in the page:

```
$("img").each(function(m){
    ...
});
```

In the body of the function, you can refer to each <img> element by index number, which is passed to you as the m parameter here. You can refer to the current element in each iteration with this keyword, so to give each <img> element an alt element "Image 1", "Image 2", and so on, you would use this code:

```
$("img").each(function(m){
  this.alt="Image " + (m + 1);
});
```

We'll put this code to work in an example.

To loop over page elements:

1. Use a text editor (such as Microsoft WordPad) to create your Web page. We'll use the example each.html from the code for the book here.

2. Enter the code to add the jQuery library and some <img> elements to the page (**Script 3.1**).

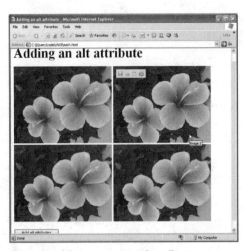

Figure 3.1 Adding new custom alt attributes.

Script 3.1 Adding <img> elements.

```
<html>
  <head>
    <title>Adding an alt attribute
    </title>
    <script type="text/javascript"
      src="http://code.jquery.com/jquery-
        latest.js">
    </script>
  </head>
  <body>
    <h1>Adding an alt attribute</h1>
    <img src="image1.jpg"></img>
    <img src="image2.jpg"></img>
    <img src="image3.jpg"></img>
    <img src="image4.jpg"></img>
    <br>
  </body>
</html>
```

Script 3.2 Looping all <img> elements.

```
<html>
  <head>
    <title>Adding an alt attribute
    </title>
    <script type="text/javascript"
      src="http://code.jquery.com/jquery-
        latest.js"></script>
    <script type="text/javascript">
      function addAlt()
      {
        $("img").each(function(m){
          this.alt="Image " + (m + 1);
        });
      }
    </script>
  </head>
  <body>
    <h1>Adding an alt attribute</h1>
    <img src="image1.jpg"></img>
    <img src="image2.jpg"></img>
    <img src="image3.jpg"></img>
    <img src="image4.jpg"></img>
    <br>
    <form>
    <input type = "button"
      value="Add alt attributes"
      onclick="addAlt()"
    </input>
    </form>
  </body>
</html>
```

3. Add the code to loop all <img> elements and add an alt attribute to each (**Script 3.2**).

4. Save the file.

5. Navigate to the file in your browser.

6. Click the button to add an alt attribute to each image, which you can see when you hover the mouse over each image (**Figure 3.1**).

LOOPING OVER ELEMENTS IN A WRAPPED SET

Reading Attribute Values

jQuery lets you examine the values of attributes with the `attr()` function.

For example, if you have two `<img>` elements in a page and want to read the `alt` attribute of the first `<img>` element, you can pass the name of the attribute to be read to the jQuery `attr()` function:

`$("img:first").attr("alt")`

In addition, jQuery provides a way of getting the elements from a jQuery wrapped set. You might think that this would work:

`$("img")[0].attr("alt")`

However, the [0] syntax returns a browser element, not a jQuery wrapped element, so the `attr()` function won't work here. An easy way of getting elements from a wrapped set is to use the jQuery `slice()` function; `slice(m, n)` returns the elements m to n-1 of a wrapped set, so you can get the first element of a wrapped set like this:

`$("img").slice(0, 1).attr("alt")`

We'll use the `slice()` function here to see how it works.

To read an attribute:

1. Use a text editor (such as Microsoft WordPad) to create your Web page. We'll use the example getattr.html from the code for the book here.

2. Enter the code to add the jQuery library and some `<img>` elements to the page (**Script 3.3**).

Script 3.3 Adding `<img>` elements to a page.

```
○ ○ ○                Script
<html>
  <head>
    <title>Reading an alt attribute
    </title>
    <script type="text/javascript"
      src="http://code.jquery.com/jquery-
        latest.js">
    </script>
  </head>
  <body>
    <h1>Reading an alt attribute</h1>
    <img src="image1.jpg"
      alt="This is an image of flowers.">
    </img>
    <img src="image2.jpg"
      alt="This is also an image of
        flowers.">
    </img>
    <br>
  </body>
</html>
```

Figure 3.2 Displaying an attribute value.

Script 3.4 Reading an alt attribute.

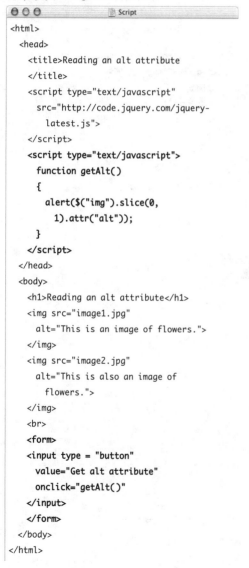

```
<html>
  <head>
    <title>Reading an alt attribute
    </title>
    <script type="text/javascript"
      src="http://code.jquery.com/jquery-
        latest.js">
    </script>
    <script type="text/javascript">
      function getAlt()
      {
        alert($("img").slice(0,
          1).attr("alt"));
      }
    </script>
  </head>
  <body>
    <h1>Reading an alt attribute</h1>
    <img src="image1.jpg"
      alt="This is an image of flowers.">
    </img>
    <img src="image2.jpg"
      alt="This is also an image of
        flowers.">
    </img>
    <br>
    <form>
    <input type = "button"
      value="Get alt attribute"
      onclick="getAlt()">
    </input>
    </form>
  </body>
</html>
```

3. Add the code to read the `alt` attribute of the first image when a button is clicked (**Script 3.4**).

4. Save the file.

5. Navigate to the file in your browser.

6. Click the button to display the first image's `alt` attribute's value (**Figure 3.2**).

Setting Attribute Values

jQuery lets you set attribute values with the attr() function as well as read them. To set an attribute value, you pass the attribute you want to add and its new value.

For example, to add an alt attribute with the value "These are flowers." to the first <img> element in a page, you can start by zeroing in on the first <img> element:

$("img:first")

Then you can set the alt attribute's value using the attr() function:

$("img:first").attr("alt", "These
 are flowers.");

Here's an example that puts this function to work.

To set an attribute:

1. Use a text editor (such as Microsoft WordPad) to create your Web page. We'll use the example setattr.html from the code for the book here.

2. Enter the code to add the jQuery library and some <img> elements to the page (**Script 3.5**).

Script 3.5 Adding two <img> elements.

```
<html>
  <head>
    <title>Setting an alt attribute
    </title>
    <script type="text/javascript"
      src="http://code.jquery.com/jquery-
        latest.js">
    </script>
  </head>

  <body>
    <h1>Setting an alt attribute</h1>
    <img src="image1.jpg">
    </img>
    <img src="image2.jpg">
    </img>
    <br>
  </body>
</html>
```

Figure 3.3 Displaying a new attribute value.

Script 3.6 Setting an alt attribute.

```
<html>
  <head>
    <title>Setting an alt attribute
    </title>
    <script type="text/javascript"
      src="http://code.jquery.com/jquery-
        latest.js">
    </script>
    <script type="text/javascript">
      function setAlt()
      {
        $("img:first").attr("alt", "These
          are flowers.");
      }
    </script>
  </head>

  <body>
    <h1>Setting an alt attribute</h1>
    <img src="image1.jpg">
    </img>
    <img src="image2.jpg">
    </img>
    <br>
    <form>
    <input type = "button"
      value="Set alt attribute"
      onclick="setAlt()"
    </input>
    </form>
  </body>
</html>
```

3. Add the code to set the `alt` attribute of the first image when a button is clicked (**Script 3.6**).

4. Save the file.

5. Navigate to the file in your browser.

6. Click the button to add an `alt` attribute to the first image (**Figure 3.3**).

✔ Tip

■ You can add nonstandard attributes to HTML elements using the `attr()` function, but if you do, your page will no longer be valid HTML.

SETTING ATTRIBUTE VALUES

Rewriting Elements' HTML

jQuery lets you rewrite elements' HTML with the html() function. All you need to do is find the elements you want to rewrite as a wrapped set and call the html() function. You pass to the html() function the new HTML text that you want to replace the current element's HTML.

For example, you can wrap all the <div> elements in a page, like this:

```
$("div")
```

Then you can replace all the <div> elements with <span> elements, like this:

```
$("div").html("<span class='blue'>" +
  "Here is a new &lt;span&gt; " +
  "element.</span>");
```

Here's an example that puts function this to work.

To rewrite an element's HTML:

1. Use a text editor (such as Microsoft WordPad) to create your Web page. We'll use the example html.html from the code for the book here.

2. Enter the code to add the jQuery library and three <div> elements to the page (**Script 3.7**).

Script 3.7 Adding three <div> elements.

```
⊖ ⊝ ⊖                    Script
<html>
<head>
  <title>Rewriting three &lt;div&gt;
    elements</title>
  <script
    src="http://code.jquery.com/jquery-
      latest.js">
  </script>
</head>

<body>
  <h1>Rewriting three &lt;div&gt;
    elements</h1>
  <div></div>
  <div></div>
  <div></div>
</body>
</html>
```

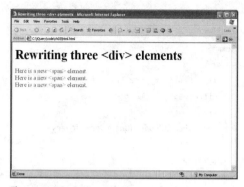

Figure 3.4 Displaying new <span> elements.

Script 3.8 Rewriting <div> elements.

```
<html>
<head>
  <title>Rewriting three &lt;div&gt;
    elements</title>
  <script
    src="http://code.jquery.com/jquery-
      latest.js">
  </script>

  <script>
  $(document).ready(function(){
    $("div").html("<span class='blue'>" +
    "Here is a new &lt;span&gt; " +
    "element.</span>");
  });
  </script>
  <style>
  .blue { color:blue; }
  </style>
</head>

<body>
  <h1>Rewriting three &lt;div&gt;
    elements</h1>
  <div></div>
  <div></div>
  <div></div>
</body>
</html>
```

3. Add the code to rewrite the HTML for the <div> elements, converting them into <span> elements as soon as the page is loaded (**Script 3.8**).

4. Save the file.

5. Navigate to the file in your browser. The <div> elements are converted to <span> elements with the text we want displayed (**Figure 3.4**).

✔ Tip

■ The html() function is handy for rewriting the HTML of elements *en masse*, unlike the standard dynamic HTML techniques available in your browser's JavaScript.

REWRITING ELEMENTS' HTML

Rewriting Elements' Text

In addition to rewriting the HTML of elements, you can use jQuery to rewrite elements' text, with the text() function. The text() function lets you replace the text inside an element, not the element's HTML.

For example, in the element

```
<h1>This is the text</h1>
```

the text is This is the text. If you use the html() function, you'll replace the whole element, including the <h1> tag, but if you use the text() function, only the contained text will be modified.

This example passes the same string passed to the html() function in the previous task (that is, "<span class='blue'>Here is a new <span>elememnt.</span>"), but this time, this text is interpreted as text, not HTML, and appears literally in the page (that is, the text this time is treated simply as text, not HTML).

To rewrite an element's text:

1. Use a text editor (such as Microsoft WordPad) to create your Web page. We'll use the example text.html from the code for the book here.

2. Enter the code to add the jQuery library and three <div> elements to the page (**Script 3.9**).

Script 3.9 Adding target <div> elements.

```
<html>
<head>
  <title>Rewriting the text of three
    &lt;div&gt; elements</title>
  <script
    src="http://code.jquery.com/jquery-
      latest.js">
  </script>
</head>

<body>
  <h1>Rewriting the text of three
    &lt;div&gt;
    elements</h1>
  <div></div>
  <div></div>
  <div></div>
</body>
</html>
```

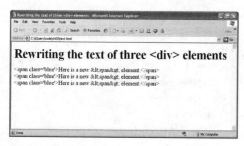

Figure 3.5 Replacing element text.

Script 3.10 Replacing elements' text.

```
Script
<html>
<head>
  <title>Rewriting the text of three
    &lt;div&gt; elements</title>
  <script
    src="http://code.jquery.com/jquery-
      latest.js">
  </script>

  <script>
  $(document).ready(function(){
    $("div").text("<span class='blue'>" +
    "Here is a new &lt;span&gt; " +
    "element.</span>");
  });
  </script>
  <style>
  .blue { color:blue; }
  </style>
</head>

<body>
  <h1>Rewriting the text of three
    &lt;div&gt;
    elements</h1>
  <div></div>
  <div></div>
  <div></div>
</body>
</html>
```

3. Add the code to set the `<div>` elements' text when the page loads (**Script 3.10**).

4. Save the file.

5. Navigate to the file in your browser. The text in the three `<div>` elements is replaced by the text we passed to the `text()` function, and the HTML markup in that text is treated as simple text, not HTML (**Figure 3.5**).

Appending Content to Elements

jQuery lets you append content to page elements with the append() function.

For example, say that you have a <p> element with this text:

```
<p>You have won </p>
```

You can locate that <p> element like this (assuming it's the only <p> element in the page):

```
$("p")
```

Then you can append other text to the <p> element like this:

```
$("p").append("<b>$1,000,000!</b>");
```

In this way, you can modify the HTML of your page on the fly.

To append content to an element:

1. Use a text editor (such as Microsoft WordPad) to create your Web page. We'll use the example append.html from the code for the book here.

2. Enter the code to add the jQuery library and a <p> element with the text "You have won " to the page (**Script 3.11**).

Script 3.11 Adding the <p> element.

```
<html>
  <head>
    <title>Appending content to a
      page</title>
    <script
      src="http://code.jquery.com/jquery-
      latest.js">
    </script>
  </head>

  <body>
    <h1>Appending content to a page</h1>
    <p>You have won </p>
  </body>
</html>
```

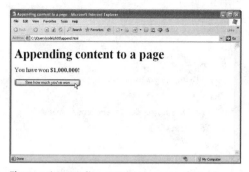

Figure 3.6 Appending content to a page element.

Script 3.12 Appending text to an element.

```
<html>
  <head>
    <title>Appending content to a
      page</title>
    <script
      src="http://code.jquery.com/jquery-
      latest.js">
    </script>

    <script>
      function addContent()
      {
    $("p").append("<b>$1,000,000!</b>");
      }
    </script>
  </head>

  <body>
    <h1>Appending content to a page</h1>
    <p>You have won </p>
    <form>
    <input type = "button"
      value="See how much you've won"
      onclick="addContent()"
    </input>
    </form>
  </body>
</html>
```

3. Add the code to append the amount the user has won when a button is clicked (**Script 3.12**).

4. Save the file.

5. Navigate to the file in your browser.

6. Click the button to make the amount the user won appear (**Figure 3.6**).

✔ Tip

■ You can also use the append() function to move existing page elements—see the next topic.

Moving Page Elements

The jQuery append( ) function is good for more than just appending new content to elements in a page—you can use the append( ) function to move elements around in a page as well.

For example, say that you have these two <p> elements:

```
<p>The first shall be last.</p>
<p>The last shall be first.</p>
```

You can use the append( ) function to move the last <p> element so that it comes before the first one. First, you get the last <p> element:

```
$("p:last")
```

Then you pass the first <p> element to the append( ) function:

```
$("p:last").append($("p:first"));
```

That does the trick—jQuery sees that you're appending an existing element, so it moves that element in the page to the new position. That reverses the order of the <p> elements:

```
<p>The last shall be first.</p>
<p>The first shall be last.</p>
```

To move a page element:

1. Use a text editor (such as Microsoft WordPad) to create your Web page. We'll use the example move.html from the code for the book here.

2. Enter the code to add the jQuery library and two <p> elements (**Script 3.13**).

Script 3.13 Adding <p> elements with text.

```
○ ○ ○                    Script
<html>
  <head>
    <title>Moving elements</title>
    <script
      src="http://code.jquery.com/jquery-
      latest.js">
    </script>
  </head>

  <body>
    <h1>Moving elements</h1>
    <p>The first shall be last.</p>
    <p>The last shall be first.</p>
  </body>
</html>
```

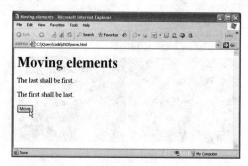

Figure 3.7 Moving a page element.

Script 3.14 Reversing the <p> elements.

```
                        Script
<html>
  <head>
    <title>Moving elements</title>
    <script
      src="http://code.jquery.com/jquery-
      latest.js">
    </script>

    <script>
      function addContent()
      {
        $("p:last").append($("p:first"));
      }
    </script>
  </head>

  <body>
    <h1>Moving elements</h1>
    <p>The first shall be last.</p>
    <p>The last shall be first.</p>
    <form>
    <input type = "button"
      value="Switch first and last paragraphs"
      onclick="addContent()"
    </input>
    </form>
  </body>
</html>
```

3. Add the code to reverse the position of the two <p> elements when a button is clicked (**Script 3.14**).

4. Save the file.

5. Navigate to the file in your browser.

6. Click the button to reverse the position of the two <p> elements (**Figure 3.7**).

MOVING PAGE ELEMENTS

Setting Element Width and Height

jQuery lets you set the width and height of elements in a page with the width() and height() functions. Using these functions is simple—you apply them to a wrapped set of elements and pass the new width or height in pixels.

To set a new width, use width():

width(*newvalue*)

To set a new height, use height():

height(*newvalue*)

This example uses the width() and height() functions to increase the width and height of two images by 50 percent at the click of a button.

To set an element's width and height:

1. Use a text editor (such as Microsoft WordPad) to create your Web page. We'll use the example width.html from the code for the book here.

2. Enter the code to add the jQuery library and two <img> elements (**Script 3.15**).

Figure 3.8 Resizing elements.

Script 3.15 Adding <img> elements with text.

```
<html>
  <head>
    <title>Setting image width and
    height
    </title>
    <script type="text/javascript"
      src="http://code.jquery.com/jquery-
        latest.js">
    </script>
  </head>
  <body>
    <h1>Setting image width and
      height</h1>
    <img src="image1.jpg"
      alt="This is an image of flowers.">
    </img>
    <img src="image2.jpg"
      alt="This is also an image of
        flowers.">
    </img>
    <br>
  </body>
</html>
```

Script 3.16 Increasing image width and height.

```
[○ ○ ○]              Script
<html>
  <head>
    <title>Setting image width and
      height
    </title>
    <script type="text/javascript"
      src="http://code.jquery.com/jquery-
        latest.js">
    </script>
    <script type="text/javascript">
      function resize()
      {
        $("img").width(486);
        $("img").height(365);
      }
    </script>
  </head>
  <body>
    <h1>Setting image width and
      height</h1>
    <img src="image1.jpg"
      alt="This is an image of flowers.">
    </img>
    <img src="image2.jpg"
      alt="This is also an image of
        flowers.">
    </img>
    <br>
    <form>
    <input type = "button"
      value="Resize"
      onclick="resize()"
    </input>
    </form>
  </body>
</html>
```

3. Add the code to increase the width and height of the two <img> elements when a button is clicked (**Script 3.16**).

4. Save the file.

5. Navigate to the file in your browser.

6. Click the button to increase the width and height of the two images as you watch (**Figure 3.8**).

SETTING ELEMENT WIDTH AND HEIGHT

Wrapping Elements

Here's something else thing you can do with jQuery wrapped sets: you can use the wrap() function to wrap all the contained elements inside other elements. This function is useful if you want to put a wrapped set of elements into, say, a <div> element for easy handling.

For example, if you have some <p> elements and want to wrap them in an <h1> header element, you can do that with the wrap() function:

```
$("p").wrap("<h1></h1>");
```

This example puts that code to work.

To wrap an element:

1. Use a text editor (such as Microsoft WordPad) to create your Web page. We'll use the example wrap.html from the code for the book here.

2. Enter the code to add the jQuery library and add four <p> elements (**Script 3.17**).

Script 3.17 Adding <p> elements to a page.

```
<html>
  <head>
    <title>Wrapping elements
    </title>
    <script type="text/javascript"
      src="http://code.jquery.com/jquery-
        latest.js">
    </script>
  </head>

  <body>
    <h1>Wrapping elements</h1>
    <p>This is paragraph 1.</p>
    <p>This is paragraph 2.</p>
    <p>This is paragraph 3.</p>
    <p>This is paragraph 4.</p>
    <br>
  </body>
</html>
```

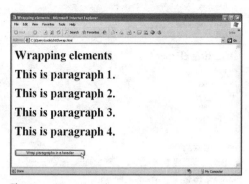

Figure 3.9 Wrapping elements.

3. Add the code to wrap the <p> elements inside an <h1> element when a button is clicked (**Script 3.18**).

4. Save the file.

5. Navigate to the file in your browser.

6. Click the button to wrap the <p> elements in an <h1> element, which makes the <p> elements headers themselves (**Figure 3.9**).

Script 3.18 Wrapping elements in a header.

```
<html>
  <head>
    <title>Wrapping elements
    </title>
    <script type="text/javascript"
      src="http://code.jquery.com/jquery-
        latest.js">
    </script>
    <script type="text/javascript">
      function wrapper()
      {
        $("p").wrap("<h1></h1>");
      }
    </script>
  </head>

  <body>
    <h1>Wrapping elements</h1>
    <p>This is paragraph 1.</p>
    <p>This is paragraph 2.</p>
    <p>This is paragraph 3.</p>
    <p>This is paragraph 4.</p>
    <br>
    <form>
    <input type = "button"
      value="Wrap paragraphs in a header"
      onclick="wrapper()"
    </input>
    </form>
  </body>
</html>
```

WRAPPING ELEMENTS

Inserting Elements

You can use the jQuery append( ) function to append elements to other elements and even move them around in a page. You can also use the before( ) and after( ) functions to insert elements with finer control.

For example, to add a new <p> element *before* an element with the ID "target", you can use this code:

```
$("#target").before("<p>New Element</p>");
```

To insert a new <p> element *after* an element with the ID "target", you can use this code:

```
$("#target").after("<p>New element</p>");
```

This example adds two new <p> elements to a set of four <p> elements.

To insert an element:

1. Use a text editor (such as Microsoft WordPad) to create your Web page. We'll use the example insert.html from the code for the book here.

2. Enter the code to add the jQuery library and four <p> elements (**Script 3.19**).

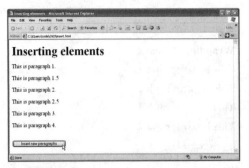

Figure 3.10 Inserting <p> elements.

Script 3.19 Adding four <p> elements to a page.

```
<html>
  <head>
    <title>Inserting elements
    </title>
    <script type="text/javascript"
      src="http://code.jquery.com/jquery-
        latest.js">
    </script>
  </head>

  <body>
    <h1>Inserting elements</h1>
    <p>This is paragraph 1.</p>
    <p id="target">This is paragraph
      2.</p>
    <p id="source">This is paragraph
      3.</p>
    <p>This is paragraph 4.</p>
    <br>
  </body>
</html>
```

Script 3.20 Inserting the <p> elements.

```
<html>
  <head>
    <title>Inserting elements
    </title>
    <script type="text/javascript"
      src="http://code.jquery.com/jquery-
        latest.js">
    </script>
    <script type="text/javascript">
      function inserter()
      {
        $("#target").before("<p>This is
          paragraph 1.5</p>");
        $("#target").after("<p>This is
          paragraph 2.5</p>");
      }
    </script>
  </head>

  <body>
    <h1>Inserting elements</h1>
    <p>This is paragraph 1.</p>
    <p id="target">This is paragraph
      2.</p>
    <p id="source">This is paragraph
      3.</p>
    <p>This is paragraph 4.</p>
    <br>
    <form>
    <input type = "button"
      value="Insert new paragraphs"
      onclick="inserter()"
    </input>
    </form>
  </body>
</html>
```

3. Add the code to insert two <p> elements (that is, paragraphs 1.5 and 2.5) when a button is clicked (**Script 3.20**).

4. Save the file.

5. Navigate to the file in your browser.

6. Click the button to add the two new <p> elements (**Figure 3.10**).

Editing the value Attribute

You can use jQuery val() function to work with the value attribute of form elements such as buttons and text fields. The value attribute holds the data corresponding to the control: for example, the text in a text field, or the caption of a button.

When you call val() without any arguments, it returns the current data in the corresponding element's value attribute.

Passing data to the val() function sets the value attribute of the corresponding element to that data. For example, to set the value attribute of an element with the ID "target" to "Hello there.", you use this code:

```
$("#target").val("Hello there.");
```

This example sets the text in a text field at the click of a button.

To edit the value attribute:

1. Use a text editor (such as Microsoft WordPad) to create your Web page. We'll use the example val.html from the code for the book here.

2. Enter the code to add the jQuery library and a text field to the page (**Script 3.21**).

Script 3.21 Adding a text field.

```
<html>
  <head>
    <title>Editing the value attribute
    </title>
    <script type="text/javascript"
      src="http://code.jquery.com/jquery-
        latest.js">
    </script>
  </head>

  <body>
    <h1>Editing the value attribute</h1>
    <br>
    <form>
    <input type = "text" id="target">
    </input>
    </form>
  </body>
</html>
```

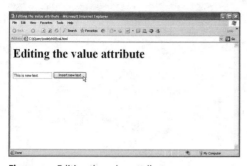

Figure 3.11 Editing the value attribute.

Script 3.22 Adding text to a text field.

```
Script
<html>
  <head>
    <title>Editing the value attribute
    </title>
    <script type="text/javascript"
      src="http://code.jquery.com/jquery-
        latest.js">
    </script>
    <script type="text/javascript">
      function inserter()
      {
        $("#target").val("This is new
          text.");
      }
    </script>
  </head>

  <body>
    <h1>Editing the value attribute</h1>
    <br>
    <form>
    <input type = "text" id="target">
    </input>
    <input type = "button"
      value="Insert new text"
      onclick="inserter()"
    </input>
    </form>
  </body>
</html>
```

3. Add the code to set the text in the text field to `("This is new text.)"` when a button is clicked (**Script 3.22**).

4. Save the file.

5. Navigate to the file in your browser.

6. Click the button to display the new text in the text field (**Figure 3.11**).

Working with Events

JavaScript is all about making your pages come alive—but you won't get very far without events.

Events let you respond to user actions such as clicks, double-clicks, mouse movements, and keystrokes. That's the kind of thing that JavaScript is good at, and it's one of the mainstays of jQuery.

Why is event handling so important in jQuery? jQuery unifies event handling in multiple browsers, whereas cross-browser event handling in straight JavaScript is a nightmare.

Event Handling in JavaScript and jQuery

If you've ever tried to support, say, drag-and-drop operations in a cross-browser way in straight JavaScript, you know the difficulties. Internet Explorer and Firefox have very different ways of handling events, from top to bottom, and you have to invest a lot of code in smoothing out the differences.

When you move the mouse, for example, an event object is created in both browsers that contains the mouse position information, such as the X and Y location of the mouse. But the way you access that event object is entirely different in the two browsers.

In both browsers, you set up JavaScript functions called *event handlers* (also called *listeners*) to execute code when the corresponding event occurs. But the way you connect event handlers to events differs between the two browsers. And the way you access the event object differs. In Internet Explorer, the event object is a subobject of another browser object, and in Firefox, the event object is passed to your event handlers.

The nightmare only begins there. You access the mouse position and other items such as the page element that the mouse is over through event object *properties*. And those properties have different names—and sometimes different meanings—depending on the browser in which your code is running.

So in addition to writing your code, you have to work with different properties. In fact, if you try to support drag-and-drop using straight JavaScript in the two browsers, you'll need to start by determining which browser the user has, and then execute entirely different code depending on the browser.

So that's double the code that you need to write, and double the testing you have to do. And you'll quickly find yourself doing this double work if you write any JavaScript beyond the most basic event handlers that just pop up an alert box on the screen.

That's where jQuery comes in. jQuery unifies event handling with a single way of attaching event handlers to page elements, a single type of event object, and a single set of event object properties. This alone is worth the price of admission.

jQuery also allows you to attach multiple event handlers to page elements and uses standard names (such as click) for events, making working with these events easier. It also makes the event object easily available to event handlers by simply passing that object to event handlers.

That's not to say that event handling in jQuery is not sophisticated. You can also cancel event bindings and create event handlers that execute only once. You can even call alternate event handlers every other time an event happens.

It all takes place in jQuery. Let's start digging into event handling now.

Binding an Event Handler to an Event

Event handling in jQuery begins by connecting an event, such as a mouse click, to an event handler. Then when the event occurs, the event handler will be called, and the code in the event handler will be executed.

You bind a page element's event to an event handler using the bind() function. For example, if a page contains an image and you want to bind one of the image's events to an event handler, you would execute code like this:

$("img").bind(*event, data, handler*)

Here, *event* is a string holding the type of event. The possible values are blur, focus, load, resize, scroll, unload, beforeunload, click, dblclick, mousedown, mouseup, mousemove, mouseover, mouseout, mouseenter, mouseleave, change, select, submit, keydown, keypress, keyup, and error.

The *data* parameter holds optional data you want passed to the event handler as the data property of the event object (you can omit this parameter), and *handler* is the event handler function.

Here, we'll see how to bind the click event of an image to an event handler that displays an alert box.

To bind an event:

1. Use a text editor (such as Microsoft WordPad) to create your Web page. We'll use the example bind.html from the code for the book here.

2. Enter the code to add the jQuery library and an <img> element to the page (**Script 4.1**).

Script 4.1 Adding an <img> element.

```
<html>
  <head>
    <title>Binding event handlers to
      events</title>
    <script
      src="http://code.jquery.com/jquery-
        latest.js">
    </script>
  </head>

  <body>
    <h1>Binding event handlers to
      events</h1>
    <h1>Click the flower...</h1>
    <img id="target" src="Image1.jpg"/>
  </body>
</html>
```

Figure 4.1 Triggering an image's click event.

Script 4.2 Binding an image's click event.

```
<html>
  <head>
    <title>Binding event handlers to
      events</title>
    <script
      src="http://code.jquery.com/jquery-
        latest.js">
    </script>

    <script>
      $(function(){
        $('#target')
          .bind('click',function(event) {
            alert('Hello!');
          });
      });
    </script>
  </head>

  <body>
    <h1>Binding event handlers to
      events</h1>
    <h1>Click the flower...</h1>
    <img id="target" src="Image1.jpg"/>
  </body>
</html>
```

3. Add the code to bind the image's click event to an event handler function that displays an alert box (**Script 4.2**).

4. Save the file.

5. Navigate to the file in your browser.

6. Click the image to display an alert box (**Figure 4.1**).

Binding Multiple Event Handlers

jQuery also allows you to bind multiple event handlers to events.

For example, you could bind three different event handler functions to a page element's click event like this, where you call the bind() function three different times:

```
$('#target')
  .bind('click',function(event) {
    alert('Hello!');
  })
  .bind('click',function(event) {
    alert('Hello again!');
  })
  .bind('click',function(event) {
    alert('Hello yet again!');
  });
```

Now when the click event occurs, the first event handler will be called, followed by the second, followed by the third.

We'll put this code to work in an example.

To bind multiple event handlers:

1. Use a text editor (such as Microsoft WordPad) to create your Web page. We'll use the example multiple.html from the code for the book here.

2. Enter the code to add the jQuery library and an <img> element to the page (**Script 4.3**).

Script 4.3 Adding one <img> element.

```
<html>
  <head>
    <title>Binding event handlers to
      events</title>
    <script
      src="http://code.jquery.com/jquery-
      latest.js">
    </script>
  </head>

  <body>
    <h1>Binding event handlers to
      events</h1>
    <h1>Click the flower...</h1>
    <img id="target" src="Image1.jpg"/>
  </body>
</html>
```

Figure 4.2 An alert box.

Script 4.4 Binding three event handlers.

```
000                    📄 Script
<html>
  <head>
    <title>Binding event handlers to
      events</title>
    <script
      src="http://code.jquery.com/jquery-
      latest.js">
    </script>

    <script>
      $(function(){
        $('#target')
          .bind('click',function(event) {
            alert('Hello!');
          })
          .bind('click',function(event) {
            alert('Hello again!');
          })
          .bind('click',function(event) {
            alert('Hello yet again!');
          });
      });
    </script>
  </head>

  <body>
    <h1>Binding event handlers to
      events</h1>
    <h1>Click the flower...</h1>
    <img id="target" src="Image1.jpg"/>
  </body>
</html>
```

3. Add the code to bind three event handlers to the image's click event (**Script 4.4**).

4. Save the file.

5. Navigate to the file in your browser.

6. Click the image, which will display a succession of alert boxes, one of which is shown in **Figure 4.2**.

Binding Event Handlers Using Shortcuts

You don't need to bind an event handler to a page event using the bind( ) function like this:

```
.bind('click',function(event) {...
```

Instead, you can use a shortcut: you can use the event name as the binding function itself. Here's how to bind the click event, for example:

```
.click(function(event) {...
```

Note the difference; you don't pass the name of the event to bind here, just the event handler function.

Here are the possible shortcut functions: blur( ), focus( ), load( ), resize( ), scroll( ), unload( ), beforeunload( ), click( ), dblclick( ), mousedown( ), mouseup( ), mousemove( ), mouseover( ), mouseout( ), mouseenter( ), mouseleave( ), change( ), select( ), submit( ), keydown( ), keypress( ), keyup( ), and error( ).

We'll put this code to work in an example; we'll bind the click event of an image to a handler function using the click( ) function.

To bind an event using a shortcut:

1. Use a text editor (such as Microsoft WordPad) to create your Web page. We'll use the example click.html from the code for the book here.

2. Enter the code to add the jQuery library and some <img> elements to the page (**Script 4.5**).

Script 4.5 Adding an <img> element as an event source.

```
<html>
  <head>
    <title>Binding event handlers using
      shortcuts</title>
    <script
      src="http://code.jquery.com/jquery-
      latest.js">
    </script>
  </head>

  <body>
    <h1>Binding event handlers using
      shortcuts</h1>
    <h1>Click the flower...</h1>
    <img id="target" src="Image1.jpg"/>
  </body>
</html>
```

Figure 4.3 Using an event binding shortcut function.

Script 4.6 Using a click( ) shortcut.

```
<html>
  <head>
    <title>Binding event handlers using
      shortcuts</title>
    <script
      src="http://code.jquery.com/jquery-
      latest.js">
    </script>

    <script>
      $(function(){
        $('#target')
          .click(function(event) {
            alert('Hello!');
          });
      });
    </script>
  </head>

  <body>
    <h1>Binding event handlers using
      shortcuts</h1>
    <h1>Click the flower...</h1>
    <img id="target" src="Image1.jpg"/>
  </body>
</html>
```

3. Add the code to connect the image's click event to an event handler function that displays an alert box using the click( ) shortcut (**Script 4.6**).

4. Save the file.

5. Navigate to the file in your browser.

6. Click the image, displaying the alert box (**Figure 4.3**).

Calling Event Handlers Only Once

You can use jQuery to bind an event to an event handler that you want to run only once. This capability is useful if you have an initialization process that needs to be executed only once. For example, you may want to initialize an online database—a process that needs to be done only one time.

To bind events to an event handler so that the event handler is run only once, you use the one() function:

.one('click',function(event) {...

Let's put this function to work.

To call an event handler only once:

1. Use a text editor (such as Microsoft WordPad) to create your Web page. We'll use the example one.html from the code for the book here.

2. Enter the code to add the jQuery library and an <img> element to the page (**Script 4.7**).

Script 4.7 Adding an <img> element.

```
<html>
  <head>
    <title>Allowing event handlers to be
      called only once</title>
    <script
      src="http://code.jquery.com/jquery-
      latest.js">
    </script>
  </head>

  <body>
    <h1>Allowing event handlers to be
      called only once</h1>
    <h1>Click the flower...</h1>
    <img id="target" src="Image1.jpg"/>
  </body>
</html>
```

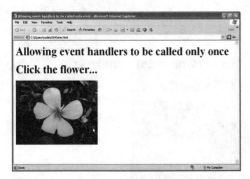

Figure 4.4 Using an event binding only once.

Script 4.8 Executing an event handler only once.

```
<html>
  <head>
    <title>Allowing event handlers to be
      called only once</title>
    <script
      src="http://code.jquery.com/jquery-
      latest.js">
    </script>

    <script>
      $(function(){
        $('#target')
          .one('click',function(event) {
            alert('Hello!');
          });
      });
    </script>
  </head>

  <body>
    <h1>Allowing event handlers to be
      called only once</h1>
    <h1>Click the flower...</h1>
    <img id="target" src="Image1.jpg"/>
  </body>
</html>
```

3. Add the code to connect the image's click event to an event handler function that will be executed only once (**Script 4.8**).

4. Save the file.

5. Navigate to the file in your browser (**Figure 4.4**).

6. Click the image, displaying an alert box.

7. Click the image again; now no alert box appears.

Unbinding Event Handlers

You can also disconnect events from event handlers using jQuery. For example, if an option is no longer available in your application, you may want to remove the click event handler that responds to events.

You can disconnect events from event handlers using the unbind() function:

```
.unbind('click',function(event) {...
```

You just need to pass the unbind() function the name of the event you're disconnecting and the event handler to which the event is currently tied.

Let's give this function a try by disconnecting a click event from an image when the image is clicked.

To unbind an event:

1. Use a text editor (such as Microsoft WordPad) to create your Web page. We'll use the example unbind.html from the code for the book here.

2. Enter the code to add the jQuery library and <img> elements to the page with a click event connected to a function named clicker() (**Script 4.9**).

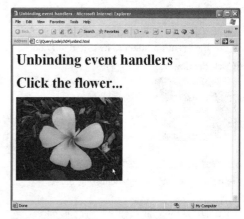

Figure 4.5 Unbinding an event handler.

Script 4.9 Connecting a click event to a handler.

```
<html>
  <head>
    <title>Unbinding event handlers</title>
    <script
    src="http://code.jquery.com/jquery-
    latest.js">
    </script>

    <script>
      $(function(){
        $('#target').bind('click',
          clicker);
      });
    </script>
  </head>

  <body>
    <h1>Unbinding event handlers</h1>
    <h1>Click the flower...</h1>
    <img id="target" src="Image1.jpg"/>
  </body>
</html>
```

Script 4.10 Unbinding a click event.

```
○ ○ ○                    Script
<html>
  <head>
    <title>Unbinding event handlers</title>
    <script
    src="http://code.jquery.com/jquery-
    latest.js">
    </script>

    <script>
      $(function(){
        $('#target').bind('click',
          clicker);
      });

      function clicker(event)
      {
        alert('Click event unbound');
        $('#target').unbind('click', \
          clicker);
      }
    </script>
  </head>

  <body>
    <h1>Unbinding event handlers</h1>
    <h1>Click the flower...</h1>
    <img id="target" src="Image1.jpg"/>
  </body>
</html>
```

3. Add the code to display an alert box in the `clicker()` function and then disconnect the click event from the `clicker()` function (**Script 4.10**).

4. Save the file.

5. Navigate to the file in your browser (**Figure 4.5**).

6. Click the image, displaying the alert box and unbinding the click event.

7. Click the image again to ensure that there's no response.

Using the Event Object

There's a great deal more power in jQuery event handling than what you've seen so far. For example, event handler functions are passed an event object, and that object has properties and methods that you can use.

For instance, if you want to know where a page element was clicked, you can use the pageX and pageY properties of the event object. If you want to know the target element of an event, you can use the event object's target property.

We'll take a look at the properties and methods of the jQuery event object in this topic and put them to work in the following topics.

Event Object Properties

Table 4.1 lists the properties of the jQuery event object.

Event Object Methods

Table 4.2 lists the event object methods.

Table 4.1

Event Object Properties	
PROPERTY	CONTAINS
event.altKey	Contains true if the Alt key was pressed.
event.ctrlKey	Contains true if the Ctrl key was pressed.
event.data	Contains the data passed to the jQuery bind( ) function.
event.keyCode	Contains the key code for the pressed key.
event.pageX	Contains the X mouse coordinates relative to the client area.
event.pageY	Contains the Y mouse coordinates relative to the client area.
event.relatedTarget	Contains the element that the mouse was previously on.
event.result	Contains the last value returned by an event handler.
event.screenX	Contains the X mouse coordinates relative to the screen.
event.screenY	Contains the Y mouse coordinates relative to the screen.
event.shiftKey	Contains true if the Shift key was pressed.
event.target	Contains the element that issued the event.
event.timeStamp	Contains the timestamp (in milliseconds) indicating when the event happened.
event.type	Contains the name of the event.

Table 4.2

Event Object Methods	
METHOD	DOES THIS
event.isDefaultPrevented( )	Returns true if event.preventDefault( ) was ever called on the event object.
event.isImmediatePropagationStopped( )	Returns true if event.stopImmediatePropagation( ) was ever called on this event object.
event.isPropagationStopped( )	Returns true if event.stopPropagation( ) was ever called on this event object.
event.preventDefault( )	Stops the browser from executing the default action for this event.
event.stopImmediatePropagation( )	Stops the remainder of the handlers from being executed.

Script 4.11 Adding an <img> element and two <p> elements.

```
                Script
<html>
  <head>
    <title>Binding event handlers to
      events</title>
    <script
    src="http://code.jquery.com/jquery-
    latest.js">
    </script>
    <script>
    $(function(){
      $('#target').bind('click',
        clicker);
    });
    </script>
  </head>
  <body>
    <h1>Binding event handlers to
      events</h1>
    <h1>Click the flower...</h1>
    <img id="target" src="Image1.jpg"/>
  </body>
</html>
```

Getting Mouse Coordinates

Mouse event objects come with built-in properties that let you determine exactly where the event occurred.

You can get the page coordinates—that is, the coordinates of the mouse event with respect to the upper-left corner of the client area (the area where the action takes place in a window, excluding toolbars, borders, the status bar, and so on) using the pageX and pageY properties. These properties are X and Y coordinates relative to the upper-left corner of the client area, which is location (0, 0).

You can also get the mouse location with respect to the upper-left corner of the screen using the screenX and screenY properties.

All coordinates are measured in pixels here.

To get a mouse event's coordinates:

1. Use a text editor (such as Microsoft WordPad) to create your Web page. We'll use the example screenxy.html from the code for the book here.

2. Enter the code to add the jQuery library and an <img> element and two <p> elements to the page (**Script 4.11**).

continues on next page

3. Add the code to display the screenX and screenY and the pageX and pageY coordinates when the mouse is clicked (**Script 4.12**).

4. Save the file.

5. Navigate to the file in your browser.

6. Click the image, displaying the page and screen coordinates of the click event (**Figure 4.6**).

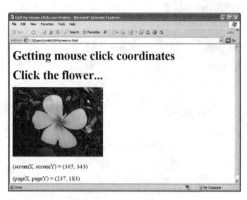

Figure 4.6 Getting mouse coordinates.

Script 4.12 Displaying mouse coordinates.

```
<html>
  <head>
    <title>Getting mouse click
      coordinates</title>
    <script
    src="http://code.jquery.com/jquery-
    latest.js">
    </script>
      <script>
      $(function(){
      $('#target').bind('click',
      clicker);
      });
      function clicker(event)
      {
    $('#p1').text('(screenX, screenY) =
    ('
    + event.screenX + ', ' +
      event.screenY +
    ')');
    $('#p2').text('(pageX, pageY) = ('
    + event.pageX + ', ' + event.pageY +
    ')');
      }
      </script>
  </head>
  <body>
    <h1>Getting mouse click
      coordinates</h1>
    <h1>Click the flower...</h1>
    <img id="target" src="Image1.jpg"/>
    <p id="p1"></p>
    <p id="p2"></p>
  </body>
</html>
```

Script 4.13 Adding an <img> element and binding its click event.

```
                    Script
<html>
  <head>
    <title>Getting event type</title>
    <script
    src="http://code.jquery.com/jquery-
    latest.js">
    </script>

    <script>
      $(function(){
      $('#target').bind('click',
        clicker);
      });
    </script>
  </head>

  <body>
    <h1>Getting event type</h1>
    <h1>Click the flower...</h1>
    <img id="target" src="Image1.jpg"/>
  </body>
</html>
```

Getting the Event Type

You can connect a single event handler to many different types of events. For example, you may want to centralize your event handling for clicks and double-clicks in one function.

How then can you determine what type of event actually occurred: a click or a double-click?

You can use the event object's type property. That property stores the name of the event in human language. The possibilities are blur, focus, load, resize, scroll, unload, before-unload, click, dblclick, mousedown, mouseup, mousemove, mouseover, mouseout, mouseenter, mouseleave, change, select, submit, keydown, keypress, keyup, and error.

Let's take a look at an event and determine its type in an example.

To get an event's type:

1. Use a text editor (such as Microsoft WordPad) to create your Web page. We'll use the example type.html from the code for the book here.

2. Enter the code to add the jQuery library to the page and connect a function named clicker() to an <img> element (**Script 4.13**).

continues on next page

3. Add the code to display the event type in a <p> element when the image is clicked (**Script 4.14**).

4. Save the file.

5. Navigate to the file in your browser.

6. Click the image, which makes the <p> element display text indicating that a click event occurred (**Figure 4.7**).

Figure 4.7 Catching a click event.

Script 4.14 Displaying the event type.

```
<html>
  <head>
    <title>Getting event type</title>
    <script
    src="http://code.jquery.com/jquery-
    latest.js">
    </script>

    <script>
      $(function(){
      $('#target').bind('click',
        clicker);
      });

      function clicker(event)
      {
    $('#p1').text('Event type: '
    + event.type);
      }
    </script>
  </head>

  <body>
    <h1>Getting event type</h1>
    <h1>Click the flower...</h1>
    <img id="target" src="Image1.jpg"/>
    <p id="p1"></p>
  </body>
</html>
```

Script 4.15 Binding the keyUp event.

```
                    Script
<html>
  <head>
    <title>Capturing key events</title>
    <script
     src="http://code.jquery.com/jquery-
     latest.js">
    </script>

    <script>
      $(function(){
      $('#target').bind('keyup', typer);
      });
    </script>
  </head>

  <body id="target">
    <h1>Capturing key events</h1>
  </body>
</html>
```

Capturing Keystrokes

You can capture keystrokes with jQuery, although it takes a little work to figure out what key was typed.

With the keyDown, keyPress, and keyUp events, the event object's keyCode property holds the struck key's code. Note that the key code holds only the raw key code, with no information about capitalization (you can check the shiftKey property for that).

We'll look at an example to get a basic idea of how to determine which key was struck when a key event occurs. To convert from the raw key code to the character that was struck, we'll use the JavaScript method String.fromCharCode() (which returns capital letters).

In this example, you can type keys, and the code will display the struck key in a <p> element.

To capture keystrokes:

1. Use a text editor (such as Microsoft WordPad) to create your Web page. We'll use the example keycode.html from the code for the book here.

2. Enter the code to add the jQuery library to the page and bind the <body> element's keyUp event to a JavaScript function (**Script 4.15**).

continues on next page

3. Add the code to display the key that was struck in a <p> element (**Script 4.16**).

4. Save the file.

5. Navigate to the file in your browser.

6. Type a character; the character you typed is echoed in the page (**Figure 4.8**).

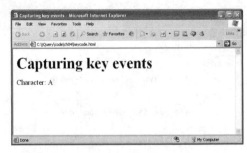

Figure 4.8 Reading keystrokes.

Script 4.16 Displaying the key that was struck.

```
<html>
  <head>
    <title>Capturing key events</title>
    <script
    src="http://code.jquery.com/jquery-
    latest.js">
    </script>

    <script>
     $(function(){
     $('#target').bind('keyup', typer);
     });

     function typer(event)
     {
       $('#p1').text('Character: '
     + String.fromCharCode(
     event.keyCode));
     }
    </script>
  </head>

  <body id="target">
    <h1>Capturing key events</h1>
    <p id="p1"></p>
  </body>
</html>
```

Script 4.17 Binding hover events.

```
<html>
  <head>
    <title>Capturing hover events</title>
    <script
      src="http://code.jquery.com/jquery-
      latest.js">
    </script>

    <script>
      $(function(){
      $('#target').hover(over, out);
      });
    </script>
  </head>

  <body>
    <h1>Capturing hover events</h1>
    <p id="target">Here is the text!</p>
  </body>
</html>
```

Capturing Hover Events

The jQuery library has a special function for handling mouse hover events, in which the mouse cursor rests on a page element. That function is hover( ):

hover(*over*, *out*)

You pass two functions to hover( ): the *over( )* function should be called when the mouse is over a page element, and the *out( )* function should be called when the mouse leaves the page element.

In this example, we'll italicize some text in a page when the mouse hovers over that text, and restore it to normal when the mouse leaves.

To capture hover events

1. Use a text editor (such as Microsoft WordPad) to create your Web page. We'll use the example hover.html from the code for the book here.

2. Enter the code to add the jQuery library to the page and a <p> element with some text in it, binding the hover events to two JavaScript functions (**Script 4.17**).

continues on next page

3. Add the code to italicize the text in the <p> element when the mouse hovers over it, and restore the text to normal when the mouse leaves (**Script 4.18**).

4. Save the file.

5. Navigate to the file in your browser.

6. Move the mouse over the text to see it turn to italics (**Figure 4.9**).

✔ Tip

■ When you want to change the style of the text in the <p> element, you don't have to access the <p> element as $('#target'), using the ID value of the <p> element. You can refer to the <p> element as event. target instead, because the target of events is passed to you in the event object; take a look at the next topic.

Figure 4.9 Italicizing text.

Script 4.18 Catching hover events.

```
<html>
  <head>
    <title>Capturing hover events</title>
    <script
      src="http://code.jquery.com/jquery-
      latest.js">
    </script>

    <script>
      $(function(){
      $('#target').hover(over, out);
      });

      function over(event)
      {
        $('#target').css("font-style",
        "italic");
      }

      function out(event)
      {
        $('#target').css("font-style",
        "normal");
      }
    </script>
  </head>

  <body>
    <h1>Capturing hover events</h1>
    <p id="target">Here is the text!</p>
  </body>
</html>
```

Script 4.19 Binding an image's click event.

```
<html>
  <head>
    <title>Getting event target</title>
    <script
      src="http://code.jquery.com/jquery-
      latest.js">
    </script>

    <script>
      $(function(){
        $('#figure1').bind('click',
        clicker);
      });
    </script>
  </head>

  <body>
    <h1>Getting event target</h1>
    <h1>Click the flower...</h1>
    <img id="figure1" src="Image1.jpg"/>
  </body>
</html>
```

Getting Event Targets

You can set up just a single event handler to handle a type of event for many different elements. For example, you may have many images in a page and want to write a click event handler for them all, saving you the need to duplicate a lot of code.

To do that, you'll need to determine from the event object the page element in which the event occurred, and you can do that with the target property of the event object.

The target property contains an object corresponding to the page element that was the target of the event. So, for example, if an image was clicked, the event object passed to its click event handler will contain an object corresponding to the image.

In this example, we'll use the event object's target property to recover and display the ID value of an image that the user clicked.

To get the event target:

1. Use a text editor (such as Microsoft WordPad) to create your Web page. We'll use the example target.html from the code for the book here.

2. Enter the code to add the jQuery library and an <img> element to the page, binding the image's click event to a JavaScript function (**Script 4.19**).

continues on next page

3. Add the code to display the ID value of the clicked image (**Script 4.20**).

4. Save the file.

5. Navigate to the file in your browser.

6. Click the image, displaying its ID value (**Figure 4.10**).

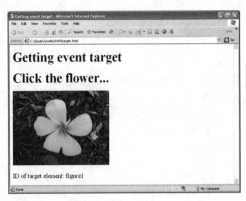

Figure 4.10 Getting an element's ID.

Script 4.20 Displaying the event target's ID.

```
<html>
  <head>
    <title>Getting event target</title>
    <script
      src="http://code.jquery.com/jquery-
      latest.js">
    </script>

    <script>
      $(function(){
        $('#figure1').bind('click',
        clicker);
      });

      function clicker(event)
      {
        $('#p1').text(
        "ID of target element: "
        + event.target.id);
      }
    </script>
  </head>

  <body>
    <h1>Getting event target</h1>
    <h1>Click the flower...</h1>
    <img id="figure1" src="Image1.jpg"/>
    <p id="p1"></p>
  </body>
</html>
```

VISUAL EFFECTS AND ANIMATION

jQuery supports the full range of visual effects and animation.

These effects can give your Web pages a very professional and dynamic appearance. This chapter shows you what jQuery has to offer.

jQuery Visual Effects Overview

This chapter starts with the basics, the show( ) and hide( ) functions, which you use to show and hide page elements. Showing and hiding is a cool effect in a Web page because space is always at a premium in Web pages, and this effect can help you display items only when needed.

You can also use the show( ) and hide( ) functions to set the duration (in milliseconds) of the showing and hiding transitions. For example, you can gradually hide a page element. You can also specify a callback function that you want called when the showing or hiding operation is complete.

A handy toggle( ) function lets you alternate between page elements, making first one visible and then the other. And as with show( ) and hide( ), you can set the duration of the transition for some very cool visual effects.

You can also perform fades, making page elements fade in and out, creating a striking visual effect in a Web page because it's something beyond the ordinary HTML.

You can use jQuery to perform slides, making page elements appear to slide around in a page and the other page elements adjust their positions to match. With the slideToggle( ) function, you can perform slides between two page elements.

In addition, the animate( ) function lets you perform custom animations, moving page elements around, changing their appearance, and more.

Now let's dig in and put these effects and more to work.

Script 5.1 Adding an <img> element.

```
<html>
  <head>
    <title>Showing and hiding
      images</title>

    <script
      src="http://code.jquery.com/jquery-
      latest.js">
    </script>

  </head>

  <body>
    <h1>Showing and hiding images</h1>
    <img id="target" src="Image1.jpg"/>

    <br>
  </body>
</html>
```

Showing and Hiding Page Elements

The most basic visual effect in jQuery consists of showing and hiding page elements at will.

You hide page elements with the `hide()` function, and you show them with the `show()` function. The process is simple.

You can execute the `show()` and `hide()` functions on entire wrapped sets at once, so that all the elements in that wrapped set disappear or appear in your Web page.

Here, we'll see how to show and hide an image of flowers with the click of a button.

To show and hide page elements:

1. Use a text editor (such as Microsoft WordPad) to create your Web page. We'll use the example showhide.html from the code for the book here.

2. Enter the code to add the jQuery library and an <img> element to the page (**Script 5.1**).

continues on next page

3. Add the code to connect two buttons to two functions, one of which shows the image and the other of which hides it (**Script 5.2**).

4. Save the file.

5. Navigate to the file in your browser (**Figure 5.1**).

6. Click the two buttons, Show and Hide, to alternately show and hide the image.

✔ Tip

■ More on show( ) and hide( ) is coming up in the next topic.

Figure 5.1 Showing and hiding an image.

Script 5.2 Showing and hiding an image.

```
<html>
  <head>
    <title>Showing and hiding
      images</title>

    <script
      src="http://code.jquery.com/jquery-
      latest.js">
    </script>

    <script>

      function showImage()
      {
        $('#target').show();
      }

      function hideImage()
      {
        $('#target').hide();
      }
    </script>

  </head>

  <body>
    <h1>Showing and hiding images</h1>
    <img id="target" src="Image1.jpg"/>

    <br>
    <form>
    <input type="button" value="Show"
      onclick="showImage()"></input>

    <input type="button" value="Hide"
      onclick="hideImage()"></input>
    </form>
  </body>
</html>
```

Script 5.3 Adding an image.

```
<html>
  <head>
    <title>Showing and hiding images with
      duration</title>
    <script
      src="http://code.jquery.com/jquery-
      latest.js">
    </script>
  </head>
  <body>
    <h1>Showing and hiding images with
      duration</h1>
    <img id="target" src="Image1.jpg"/>
    <br>
  </body>
</html>
```

Showing and Hiding Elements with Duration

jQuery gives you more control over showing and hiding page elements: you can set the amount of time taken for a page element to appear or disappear, and you can call a function when the transition is complete.

Here's how to use show( ) if you want to set a duration and a callback function (both of which are optional):

show(*duration*, *callback*)

Here, *duration* is the amount of time taken to show the image (in milliseconds), and *callback* is a callback function jQuery will call when the transition is complete.

The corresponding version of hide( ) looks like this:

hide(*duration*, *callback*)

Here, we'll show and hide an image, taking 2 seconds for each transition, and have jQuery call a callback function to display the text, "Hey, where did it go?" when the image is hidden.

To show and hide page elements with duration:

1. Use a text editor (such as Microsoft WordPad) to create your Web page. We'll use the example showhidespeed.html from the code for the book here.

2. Enter the code to add the jQuery library and an <img> element to the page (**Script 5.3**).

continues on next page

3. Add the code to show or hide the image with a duration of 2 seconds, and call a callback function that will display a message when the image is hidden (**Script 5.4**).

4. Save the file.

5. Navigate to the file and click a button to show or hide the image (**Figure 5.2**).

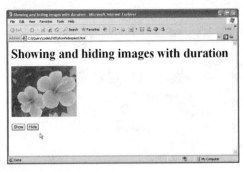

Figure 5.2 Hiding an image.

SHOWING AND **H**IDING **E**LEMENTS WITH **D**URATION

Script 5.4 Showing or hiding with duration.

```
<html>
  <head>
    <title>Showing and hiding images with
      duration</title>
    <script
      src="http://code.jquery.com/jquery-
      latest.js">
    </script>
    <script>
      function showImage()
      {
        $('#target').show(2000);
      }
      function hideImage()
      {
        $('#target').hide(2000, hey);
      }
      function hey()
      {
        $('#p1').text("Hey, where did it go?");
      }
    </script>
  </head>
```

Script 5.4 *continued*

```
  <body>
    <h1>Showing and hiding images with
      duration</h1>
    <img id="target" src="Image1.jpg"/>
    <br>
    <form>
    <input type="button" value="Show"
      onclick="showImage()"></input>
    <input type="button" value="Hide"
      onclick="hideImage()"></input>
    </form>
    <br>
    <p id="p1"></p>
  </body>
</html>
```

Script 5.5 Adding two headers.

```
                    Script
<html>
  <head>
    <title>Toggling visibility</title>
    <script
      src="http://code.jquery.com/jquery-
      latest.js">
    </script>

  </head>

  <body>
    <h1>Toggling visibility</h1>

    <h2>Now you see me.</h2>
    <h2 style="display: none">Now you
      don't.</h2>

  </body>
</html>
```

Toggling Element Visibility

jQuery has a handy function that lets you show an element if it's hidden, or hide it if it's visible: the `toggle()` function. This function is particularly useful when you have a two-state item, such as a red or green stop and go icon.

You often use `toggle()` on pairs of page elements, one of which starts out hidden, and the other visible. Then when you toggle the pair of elements, the hidden one appears and the visible one is hidden.

That's what we'll do in this example, where we'll toggle the visibility of two <h2> headers. One header (the originally visible one) reads "Now you see me." The other (originally hidden) header reads "Now you don't." By clicking a button, you'll be able to alternate between these two headers.

To toggle element visibility:

1. Use a text editor (such as Microsoft WordPad) to create your Web page. We'll use the example toggle.html from the code for the book here.

2. Enter the code to add the jQuery library to the page and then two <h2> headers, one of which is originally hidden (**Script 5.5**).

continues on next page

3. Add the code to alternate the visibility of the two headers using `toggle()` when the user clicks a button (**Script 5.6**).

4. Save the file.

5. Navigate to the file in your browser.

6. Click the button to alternate between the "Now you see me." header and the "Now you don't." header (**Figure 5.3**).

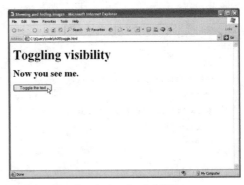

Figure 5.3 Toggling the headers' visibility.

Script 5.6 Toggling headers.

```
<html>
  <head>
    <title>Toggling visibility</title>
    <script
      src="http://code.jquery.com/jquery-
      latest.js">
    </script>

    <script>
      $(document).ready(function(){

        $("button").click(function()
        {
          $("h2").toggle();
        });
      });
    </script>
  </head>

  <body>
    <h1>Toggling visibility</h1>

    <h2>Now you see me.</h2>
    <h2 style="display: none">Now you
      don't.</h2>

    <button>Toggle the text</button>
  </body>
</html>
```

Script 5.7 Adding two headers to a page.

```
                    Script
<html>
  <head>
    <title>Toggling visibility with
      duration</title>
    <script
      src="http://code.jquery.com/jquery-
      latest.js">
    </script>

  </head>

  <body>
    <h1>Toggling visibility with
      duration</h1>

    <h2>Now you see me.</h2>
    <h2 style="display: none">Now you
      don't.</h2>

  </body>
</html>
```

Toggling Element Visibility with Duration

You can also toggle elements' visibility at a specified speed, and you can have jQuery call a callback function when the toggle operation is completed.

To toggle an element from visible to invisible or the other way around with a specific speed and a callback function, use this form of `toggle()`:

`toggle(duration, callback)`

Here, *duration* is the time in milliseconds that the toggle operation should take, and *callback* is a callback function that jQuery will call when the operation is complete.

Both parameters are optional.

We'll add a duration to the previous topic's `toggle()` example here, making the transition from hidden to visible or visible to hidden take 2 seconds.

To toggle element visibility with duration:

1. Use a text editor (such as Microsoft WordPad) to create your Web page. We'll use the example togglespeed.html from the code for the book here.

2. Enter the code to add the jQuery library to the page and then two <h2> headers, one of which is originally hidden (**Script 5.7**).

continues on next page

TOGGLING ELEMENT VISIBILITY WITH DURATION

111

3. Add the code to alternate the visibility of the two headers using `toggle( )`, specifying a duration of 2 seconds for the effect, when the user clicks a button (**Script 5.8**).

4. Save the file.

5. Navigate to the file in your browser.

6. Click the button to alternate between the "Now you see me." header and the "Now you don't." header (**Figure 5.4**). The transition takes 2 seconds.

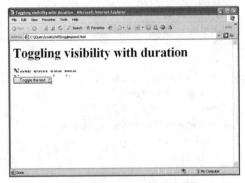

Figure 5.4 Toggling the headers' visibility with duration.

Script 5.8 Toggling headers from visible to invisible and back again.

```
<html>
  <head>
    <title>Toggling visibility with
      duration</title>
    <script
      src="http://code.jquery.com/jquery-
      latest.js">
    </script>

    <script>
      $(document).ready(function(){

        $("button").click(function()
        {
          $("h2").toggle(2000);
        });
      });
    </script>
  </head>
  <body>
    <h1>Toggling visibility with
      duration</h1>

    <h2>Now you see me.</h2>
    <h2 style="display: none">Now you
      don't.</h2>

    <button>Toggle the text</button>
  </body>
</html>
```

Script 5.9 Adding an image.

```
<html>
  <head>
    <title>Fading an image out</title>
    <script
      src="http://code.jquery.com/jquery-
      latest.js">
    </script>
  </head>

  <body>
    <h1>Fading an image out</h1>
    <img id="target" src="Image1.jpg"/>
    <br>
  </body>
</html>
```

Fading Elements Out

Here's another cool visual effect: you can make page elements fade out as the user watches. For this purpose, you can use the fadeOut( ) function:

fadeOut(*duration*, *callback*)

In this case, *duration* is the time in milliseconds that the fading operation should take, and *callback* is a callback function that jQuery will call when the operation is complete.

Both parameters are optional.

In this example, we'll make an image fade out when the user clicks a button.

To fade out an element:

1. Use a text editor (such as Microsoft WordPad) to create your Web page. We'll use the example fadeout.html from the code for the book here.

2. Enter the code to add the jQuery library to the page and an <img> element that is originally hidden (**Script 5.9**).

continues on next page

3. Add the code to make the image fade out when the user clicks a button (**Script 5.10**).

4. Save the file.

5. Navigate to the file in your browser.

6. Click the button to make the image fade out (**Figure 5.5**).

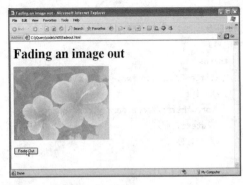

Figure 5.5 Fading out an image.

Script 5.10 Fading out an image.

```
<html>
  <head>
    <title>Fading an image out</title>
    <script
      src="http://code.jquery.com/jquery-
      latest.js">
    </script>

    <script>
      function fade()
      {
        $('#target').fadeOut(2000);
      }

    </script>
  </head>

  <body>
    <h1>Fading an image out</h1>
    <img id="target" src="Image1.jpg"/>
    <br>
    <form>
    <input type="button" value="Fade Out"
      onclick="fade()"></input>
    </form>
  </body>
</html>
```

Script 5.11 Adding a hidden image.

```
                    Script
<html>
  <head>
    <title>Fading an image in</title>
    <script
      src="http://code.jquery.com/jquery-
      latest.js">
    </script>
  </head>

  <body>
    <h1>Fading an image in</h1>
    <img id="target" src="Image1.jpg"
    style="display: none"/>
    <br>
  </body>
</html>
```

Fading Elements In

You can also fade elements in: they start out invisible and then gradually appear. To fade in elements, you can use the `fadeIn()` function:

`fadeIn(duration, callback)`

In this case, *duration* is the time in milliseconds that the fading operation should take, and *callback* is a callback function that jQuery will call when the operation is complete.

Both parameters are optional.

In this example, we'll make an image that was originally hidden fade in when the user clicks a button.

To fade in an element:

1. Use a text editor (such as Microsoft WordPad) to create your Web page. We'll use the example fadein.html from the code for the book here.

2. Enter the code to add the jQuery library to the page and then add an image that is originally hidden (**Script 5.11**).

continues on next page

3. Add the code to fade the hidden image into visibility (**Script 5.12**).

4. Save the file.

5. Navigate to the file in your browser.

6. Click the button and watch the image fade in (**Figure 5.6**).

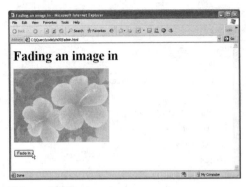

Figure 5.6 Fading in an image.

Script 5.12 Fading in an image.

```
<html>
  <head>
    <title>Fading an image in</title>
    <script
      src="http://code.jquery.com/jquery-
      latest.js">
    </script>

    <script>
      function fade()
      {
        $('#target').fadeIn(2000);
      }

    </script>
  </head>

  <body>
    <h1>Fading an image in</h1>
    <img id="target" src="Image1.jpg"
    style="display: none"/>
    <br>
    <form>
    <input type="button" value="Fade In"
      onclick="fade()"></input>
    </form>
  </body>
</html>
```

Script 5.13 Adding three <p> elements.

```
<html>
  <head>
    <title>Sliding elements up</title>
    <script type="text/javascript"
      src="http://code.jquery.com/jquery-
      latest.js">
    </script>
  </head>

  <body>
    <h1>Sliding elements up</h1>
    <div>
      <p id="first">Here is some
        text.</p>
      <p>This is also text.</p>
      <p>And here's some more text.</p>
    </div>
  </body>
</html>
```

Sliding Elements Up

You can also make page elements slide around at will. For example, the slideUp() function lets you slide page elements up, moving them from visible to invisible.

You create this effect with the slideUp() function like this:

slideUp(*duration*, *callback*)

In this case, *duration* is the time in milliseconds that the slide operation should take, and *callback* is a callback function that jQuery will call when the operation is complete.

Both parameters are optional.

In this example, we'll slide a paragraph of text up when the user clicks a button.

To slide an element up:

1. Use a text editor (such as Microsoft WordPad) to create your Web page. We'll use the example slideup.html from the code for the book here.

2. Enter the code to add the jQuery library to the page and then add three <p> elements, giving the first one the ID "first" (**Script 5.13**).

continues on next page

3. Add the code to slide the top <p> element up when the user clicks a button (**Script 5.14**).

4. Save the file.

5. Navigate to the file in your browser.

6. Click the button to make the first <p> element slide up and out of view (**Figure 5.7**).

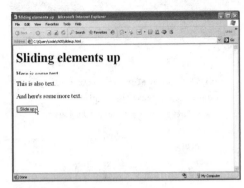

Figure 5.7 Sliding a <p> element up.

Script 5.14 Sliding a <p> element up.

```
<html>
  <head>
    <title>Sliding elements up</title>
    <script type="text/javascript"
      src="http://code.jquery.com/jquery-
      latest.js">
    </script>
    <script type="text/javascript">
      function slideup()
      {
        $('#first').slideUp("slow");
      }
    </script>
  </head>

  <body>
    <h1>Sliding elements up</h1>
    <div>
      <p id="first">Here is some
        text.</p>
      <p>This is also text.</p>
      <p>And here's some more text.</p>
    </div>
    <form>
    <input type = "button"
      value="Slide up"
      onclick="slideup()"
    </input>
    </form>

  </body>
</html>
```

Script 5.15 Adding <p> elements to a page.

```
○ ○ ○              Script
<html>
  <head>
    <title>Sliding elements up and
      down</title>
    <script type="text/javascript"
      src="http://code.jquery.com/jquery-
      latest.js">
    </script>
  </head>
  <body>
    <h1>Sliding elements up and down</h1>
    <div>
      <p id="first">Here is some
        text.</p>
      <p>This is also text.</p>
      <p>And here's some more text.</p>
    </div>
  </body>
</html>
```

Sliding Elements Down

Besides making elements slide up, you can make elements slide down. You create this effect with the slideDown() function:

slideDown(*duration*, *callback*)

In this case, *duration* is the time in milliseconds that the slide operation should take, and *callback* is a callback function that jQuery will call when the operation is complete.

Both parameters are optional.

In this example, we'll slide a paragraph of text both up and down at the click of a button.

To slide an element down:

1. Use a text editor (such as Microsoft WordPad) to create your Web page. We'll use the example slidedown.html from the code for the book here.

2. Enter the code to add the jQuery library to the page and then add three <p> elements, giving the first one the ID "first" (**Script 5.15**).

continues on next page

3. Add the code to slide the top <p> element up when the user clicks a button and down when the user clicks another button (**Script 5.16**).

4. Save the file.

5. Navigate to the file in your browser.

6. Click the first button to make the first <p> element slide up and the second button to make the element slide down again (**Figure 5.8**).

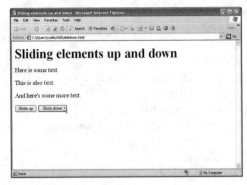

Figure 5.8 Sliding a <p> element up and down.

Script 5.16 Sliding elements up and down.

```
<html>
  <head>
    <title>Sliding elements up and
      down</title>
    <script type="text/javascript"
      src="http://code.jquery.com/jquery-
      latest.js">
    </script>
    <script type="text/javascript">
      function slideup()
      {
        $('#first').slideUp("slow");
      }
      function slidedown()
      {
        $('#first').slideDown("slow");
      }
    </script>
  </head>
```

Script 5.16 *continued*

```
<body>
    <h1>Sliding elements up and down</h1>
    <div>
      <p id="first">Here is some
        text.</p>
      <p>This is also text.</p>
      <p>And here's some more text.</p>
    </div>
  <form>
  <input type = "button"
    value="Slide up"
    onclick="slideup()"
  </input>

  <input type = "button"
    value="Slide down"
    onclick="slidedown()"
  </input>
  </form>
  </body>
</html>
```

Script 5.17 Adding new <p> elements.

```
<html>
<head>
  <title>Toggling slide
    operations</title>
  <script
    src="http://code.jquery.com/jquery-
    latest.js">
  </script>
</head>

<body>
  <h1>Toggling slide operations</h1>
    <div>
      <p id="first">Here is some
        text.</p>
      <p>This is also text.</p>
      <p>And here's some more text.</p>
    </div>
</body>
</html>
```

Toggling Sliding Operations

In addition to sliding elements up and down as you've seen in the previous two topics, you can toggle elements, sliding them up and down with the slideToggle() function. This function lets you slide an element up if it's down, and down if it's up.

You create this effect with the slideToggle() function like this:

slideToggle(*duration*, *callback*)

In this case, *duration* is the time in milliseconds that the slide operation should take, and *callback* is a callback function that jQuery will call when the operation is complete.

Both parameters are optional.

In this example, we'll slide a paragraph of text up or down when the user clicks a button.

To toggle a sliding operation:

1. Use a text editor (such as Microsoft WordPad) to create your Web page. We'll use the example slidetoggle.html from the code for the book here.

2. Enter the code to add the jQuery library to the page and then add three <p> elements, giving the first one the ID "first" (**Script 5.17**).

continues on next page

3. Add the code to slide the top <p> element up if it's down and down if it's up when the user clicks a button (**Script 5.18**).

4. Save the file.

5. Navigate to the file in your browser.

6. Click the button to make the first <p> element slide up or down (**Figure 5.9**).

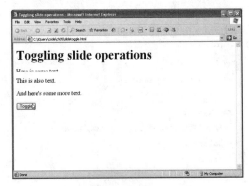

Figure 5.9 Toggling a <p> element up or down.

Script 5.18 Toggling an element up or down.

```
<html>
<head>
  <title>Toggling slide
    operations</title>
  <script
    src="http://code.jquery.com/jquery-
    latest.js">
  </script>

  <script>
$(document).ready(function(){

    $("button").click(function () {
      $("#first").slideToggle("slow");
    });

  });
  </script>
</head>

<body>
  <h1>Toggling slide operations</h1>
    <div>
      <p id="first">Here is some
        text.</p>
      <p>This is also text.</p>
      <p>And here's some more text.</p>
    </div>
  <form>
    <button>Toggle</button>
  </form>
</body>
</html>
```

Script 5.19 Adding an image.

```
                    Script
<html>
  <head>
    <title>Partially fading an
      image</title>
    <script
      src="http://code.jquery.com/jquery-
      latest.js">
    </script>
  </head>

  <body>
    <h1>Partially fading an image</h1>
    <img id="target" src="Image1.jpg"/>
    <br>
  </body>
</html>
```

Partially Fading Elements

You can use the fadeOut( ) function to fade an element out and the fadeIn( ) function to fade an element into view. You can also fade an element only partially, leaving it still partially visible, although faded.

You create this effect with the fadeTo( ) function:

fadeTo(*duration*, *opacity*, *callback*)

In this case, *duration* is the time in milliseconds that the slide operation should take, *opacity* is the final opacity of the element (0 to 1), and *callback* is a callback function that jQuery will call when the operation is complete.

All parameters are optional.

In this example, we'll fade an image to 0.333 opacity, so it will be mostly gone but still visible.

To fade an element partially:

1. Use a text editor (such as Microsoft WordPad) to create your Web page. We'll use the example fadeto.html from the code for the book here.

2. Enter the code to add the jQuery library to the page and then add an image (**Script 5.19**).

3. Add the code to fade the image partially when the user clicks a button (**Script 5.20**).

4. Save the file.

5. Navigate to the file in your browser.

6. Click the button to make the image fade out partially (**Figure 5.10**).

Figure 5.10 Fading an image partially.

Script 5.20 Partially fading an image.

```
<html>
  <head>
    <title>Partially fading an
      image</title>
    <script
      src="http://code.jquery.com/jquery-
      latest.js">
    </script>

    <script>
      function fade()
      {
        $('#target').fadeTo(2000, 0.333);
      }

    </script>
  </head>

  <body>
    <h1>Partially fading an image</h1>
    <img id="target" src="Image1.jpg"/>
    <br>
    <form>
    <input type="button" value="Fade"
      onclick="fade()"></input>
    </form>
  </body>
</html>
```

Script 5.21 Adding a <div> element.

```
⊖ ⊙ ⊙              📄 Script
<html>
  <head>
    <script
      src="http://code.jquery.com/jquery-
      latest.js"></script>

    <style>
      div {
        background-color:cyan;
        width:100px;
        border:1px solid blue;
      }
    </style>
  </head>

  <body>
    <h1>Creating custom animation</h1>
    <div id="target">Expand me</div>
    <br>
  </body>
</html>
```

Creating Custom Animation

You can create custom animation in jQuery with the *animate()* function:

animate(*params*, *duration*, *easing*, *callback*)

In this case, *params* contains the final properties of the object you're animating, such as CSS properties, *duration* is the optional time in milliseconds that the animation should take, *easing* is an optional easing function (which can determine how the animation progresses), and *callback* is an optional callback function.

In this example, we'll animate a <div> element, expanding it when the user clicks a button.

To create custom animation:

1. Use a text editor (such as Microsoft WordPad) to create your Web page. We'll use the example animate.html from the code for the book here.

2. Enter the code to add the jQuery library to the page and then add a <div> element with the text "Expand me" (**Script 5.21**).

continues on next page

3. Add the call to `animate()`, passing it the final CSS properties you want the `<div>` to have when the animation occurs after the user clicks a button (**Script 5.22**).

4. Save the file.

5. Navigate to the file in your browser.

6. Click the button to make the `<div>` element expand (**Figure 5.11**).

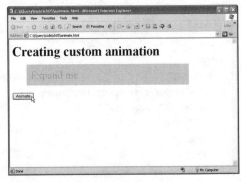

Figure 5.11 Animating the expansion of a `<div>` element.

Script 5.22 Creating a custom animation.

```
<html>
  <head>
    <script
      src="http://code.jquery.com/jquery-
      latest.js"></script>

    <script>
      function animator()
      {
        $("#target").animate({
          width: "80%",
          opacity: 0.333,
          fontSize: "26pt",
          marginLeft: "0.5in",
          borderWidth: "15px"
        }, 2000 );
      }
    </script>

    <style>
      div {
        background-color:cyan;
        width:100px;
        border:1px solid blue;
      }
    </style>
  </head>

  <body>
    <h1>Creating custom animation</h1>
    <div id="target">Expand me</div>
    <br>
    <form>
    <button
    onclick="animator()">Animate</button>
    </form>
  </body>
</html>
```

THE JQUERY
UTILITY FUNCTIONS

jQuery has a number of utility functions built in to make everyday JavaScript tasks easier. These functions are named `jquery.XXX()`, where *XXX()* is the name of the function. You can also refer to them as `$.XXX()`.

For example, the `$.trim()` function trims spaces from strings.

The utility functions can't really be categorized. They are just a group of useful functions that jQuery offers to augment JavaScript—to make tasks in JavaScript easier. You could duplicate what they do in JavaScript yourself, but it takes far less time to use a utility function.

Examples of jQuery Utility Functions

jQuery offers many utility functions that work with arrays, such as the `$.isArray()` function; you pass this function an array, and it returns true if the object you passed is an array. You can create new arrays with the `$.makeArray()` function, or get the unique members of an array with the `$.unique()` function.

Another utility function, `$.each()`, mimics the popular each loop in other programming languages (which JavaScript lacks). This function lets you loop over all the members of an object (such as an array) automatically—you don't need to set the loop index yourself.

The utility functions also include some variables, such as `$.browser`, which tells you what browser the user has and the version of that browser. By determining what browser the user has, you can tailor your HTML accordingly.

Recently, jQuery added the `$.support()` function to augment browser support. This functions lets you check whether various browser features are available in the browser that the user is using. That way, you don't have to know yourself which browser supports which features—you can just check with `$.support()`.

Let's take a look at the jQuery utility functions now.

Script 6.1 Creating a JavaScript object.

```
○○○                    Script
<html>
  <head>
    <title>Looping over an object with
      $.each()</title>
    <script
      src="http://code.jquery.com/jquery-
      latest.js">
    </script>
    <script>
      $(document).ready(function()
      {
        var obj = { one:1, two:2,
          three:3, four:4, five:5 };
    </script>
  </head>
  <body>
    <h1>Looping over an object with
      $.each()</h1>
    <div id="one"></div>
    <div id="two"></div>
    <div id="three"></div>
    <div id="four"></div>
    <div id="five"></div>
  </body>
</html>
```

Looping over Object Members with $.each( )

jQuery has a handy utility function that lets you loop over the members of a JavaScript object.

The $.each( ) function automatically loops over all members of an object for you. For example, in the body of the loop

```
$.each(obj, function(i, val) {
}
```

you can refer to the current object member by name as i, and its value as val.

Using $.each( ) saves you from having to know the name of each object member to access it; using $.each( ), you can loop over every member automatically.

In this example, we'll create a JavaScript object and then loop over all its members, displaying those members and their values.

To loop over object members:

1. Use a text editor (such as Microsoft WordPad) to create your Web page. We'll use the example each.html from the code for the book here.

2. Enter the code to add the jQuery library to the page and create an object with five members (the first member is named one with a value of 1, and so on) as well as five <div> elements (**Script 6.1**).

continues on next page

LOOPING OVER OBJECT MEMBERS WITH $.EACH()

3. Add the code to loop over all the object members and display their names and values in a `<div>` element (**Script 6.2**),

4. Save the file.

5. Navigate to the file in your browser, which should appear as shown in **Figure 6.1**, with all the object members and values displayed.

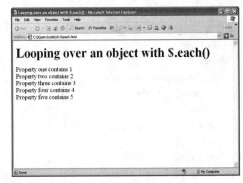

Figure 6.1 Displaying object members.

Script 6.2 Displaying object members.

```html
<html>
  <head>
    <title>Looping over an object with
      $.each()</title>
    <script
      src="http://code.jquery.com/jquery-
      latest.js">
    </script>
    <script>
      $(document).ready(function()
      {
        var obj = { one:1, two:2,
          three:3, four:4, five:5 };
        $.each(obj, function(i, val) {
          $("#" + i).append(
          document.createTextNode(
          "Property " + i + " contains "
          + val));
        });
      });
    </script>
  </head>
  <body>
    <h1>Looping over an object with
      $.each()</h1>
    <div id="one"></div>
    <div id="two"></div>
    <div id="three"></div>
    <div id="four"></div>
    <div id="five"></div>
  </body>
</html>
```

Script 6.3 Adding the jQuery library.

```
 ⊖ ○ ⊖                    📄 Script
<html>
  <head>
    <title>Determining browser
      information</title>
    <script
      src="http://code.jquery.com/jquery-
      latest.js">
    </script>
  </head>

  <body>
    <h1>Determining browser
      information</h1>
  </body>
</html>
```

Determining Browser Type with $.browser

A useful variable that comes with the utility functions is $.browser. This variable contains an object that has these properties:

◆ safari

◆ opera

◆ msie

◆ mozilla

◆ version

The first four properties hold a value of true if your code is executing in the corresponding browser, and false otherwise. The version property holds the browser's version number as a text string.

The example here displays the name and version number of the browser in which the code is running.

To determine browser type and version:

1. Use a text editor (such as Microsoft WordPad) to create your Web page. We'll use the example browser.html from the code for the book here.

2. Enter the code to add the jQuery library to the page (**Script 6.3**).

continues on next page

3. Add the code to loop over and display the $.browser properties (**Script 6.4**).

4. Save the file.

5. Navigate to the file in your browser, and you'll see the browser information (**Figure 6.2**).

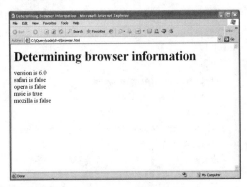

Figure 6.2 Displaying browser information.

Script 6.4 Displaying the $.browser properties.

```
<html>
  <head>
    <title>Determining browser
      information</title>
    <script
      src="http://code.jquery.com/jquery-
      latest.js">
    </script>
    <script>
      $(document).ready(function(){

        $.each($.browser,
          function(i, val) {
        $("<div>" + i + " is " + val +
        "</div>")
        .appendTo(document.body);
        });
      });
    </script>
  </head>

  <body>
    <h1>Determining browser
      information</h1>
  </body>
</html>
```

Script 6.5 Adding a <div> element.

```
○ ○ ○                Script
<html>
  <head>
    <title>Writing HTML depending on
      browser</title>
    <script
    src="http://code.jquery.com/jquery-
    latest.js">
    </script>
  </head>

  <body>
    <h1>Writing HTML depending on
      browser</h1>
    <div id="target"></div>
  </body>
</html>
```

Customizing HTML by Browser Type

The HTML that a browser supports varies by browser. To write HTML that works for a particular browser, you can check the browser type first.

For example, the <marquee> element, which displays text in a marquee scrolling across the page, is available only in Internet Explorer. The example here lets you check to see if the user has Internet Explorer before you write a <marquee> element for a page.

To customize HTML by browser type:

1. Use a text editor (such as Microsoft WordPad) to create your Web page. We'll use the example marquee.html from the code for the book here.

2. Enter the code to add the jQuery library and a <div> element to the page (**Script 6.5**).

continues on next page

3. Add the code to check whether your code is running in Internet Explorer and, if so, write a <marquee> element (**Script 6.6**).

4. Save the file.

5. Navigate to the file in Internet Explorer to see the new <marquee> element (**Figure 6.3**). The second line of text in the figure is scrolling across the screen, although you can't see that in the figure.

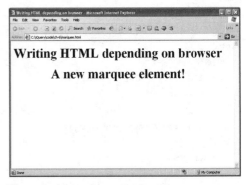

Figure 6.3 A new <marquee> element.

Script 6.6 Writing a <marquee> element.

```
<html>
  <head>
    <title>Writing HTML depending on
      browser</title>
    <script
    src="http://code.jquery.com/jquery-
    latest.js">
    </script>

    <script>
      $(document).ready(function()
      {
        if($.browser.msie) {
        $("#target").html("<marquee><h1>"
        +
          "A new marquee
          element!</h1></marquee>");
        }
      });
    </script>
  </head>

  <body>
    <h1>Writing HTML depending on
      browser</h1>
    <div id="target"></div>
  </body>
</html>
```

Checking Browser Support for Specific Features

The `$.support()` utility function returns information about supported features in the user's browser. You use it like this: `$.support. XXX`, where *XXX* is a flag with the following possible values:

◆ `boxModel`: Is true if the browser supports the W3C CSS box model.

◆ `cssFloat`: Is true if `style.cssFloat` is used to access the current CSS float value.

◆ `hrefNormalized`: Is true if the browser doesn't alter the results of `getAttribute("href")`.

◆ `htmlSerialize`: Is true if the browser properly serializes links when `innerHTML` is used.

◆ `leadingWhitespace`: Is true if the browser preserves leading white space with `innerHTML`.

◆ `noCloneEvent`: Is true if the browser does not clone event handlers when elements are cloned.

◆ `objectAll`: Is true if running `getElementsByTagName()` on an element returns all descendant elements.

◆ `opacity`: Is true if a browser can interpret the `opacity` style property.

◆ `scriptEval`: Is true if `appendChild/ createTextNode` executes scripts.

◆ `style`: Is true if `getAttribute("style")` returns the correct inline style.

◆ `tbody`: Is true if the browser allows table elements without `tbody` elements.

To check browser support:

1. Use a text editor (such as Microsoft WordPad) to create your Web page. We'll use the example support.html from the code for the book here.

2. Enter the code to add the jQuery library and an <div> element to the page (**Script 6.7**).

Script 6.7 Adding a new <div> element.

```
<html>
  <head>
    <title>Checking browser
      support</title>
    <script
      src="http://code.jquery.com/jquery-
      latest.js">
    </script>
  </head>
  <body>
    <h1>Checking browser support</h1>
    <p>
    </p>
  </body>
</html>
```

Figure 6.4 Checking support for the box model.

Script 6.8 Checking the box model.

```
<html>
  <head>
    <title>Checking browser
      support</title>
    <script
      src="http://code.jquery.com/jquery-
      latest.js">
    </script>
    <script>
    $(document).ready(function()
    {
      if($.support.boxModel){
        $("p").html("I support the W3C
          box model.");
      }
      else {
        $("p").html("I do not support
          the W3C box model.");
      }

    });
    </script>
  </head>
  <body>
    <h1>Checking browser support</h1>
    <p>
    </p>
  </body>
</html>
```

3. Add the code to check for support for the W3C box model and display the results (**Script 6.8**).

4. Save the file.

5. Navigate to the file in Firefox to verify that the browser supports the W3C box model (**Figure 6.4**).

Creating Arrays

JavaScript is full of all kinds of collections: lists, maps, named node maps, and more. You can convert such objects into standard JavaScript arrays with the handy $.makeArray() function. Arrays are usually much easier to deal with than collections.

In this example, we'll convert the list of elements returned by the JavaScript getElementsById() into an array. Then we'll reverse the array and display the resulting ordered elements in a page.

To create an array:

1. Use a text editor (such as Microsoft WordPad) to create your Web page. We'll use the example makearray.html from the code for the book here.

2. Enter the code to add the jQuery library to the page and four <p> elements with text in them (**Script 6.9**).

Script 6.9 Adding four <p> elements.

```
<html>
  <head>
    <title>Creating an array</title>
    <script
      src="http://code.jquery.com/jquery-
      latest.js">
    </script>
  </head>

  <body>
    <h1>Creating an array</h1>
    <p>Now</p>
    <p>is</p>
    <p>the</p>
    <p>time</p>
  </body>
</html>
```

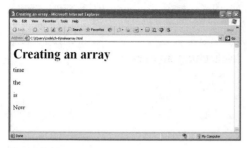

Figure 6.5 A new array.

Script 6.10 Creating an array.

```
<html>
  <head>
    <title>Creating an array</title>
    <script
      src="http://code.jquery.com/jquery-
      latest.js">
    </script>

    <script>
      $(document).ready(function()
      {

        var array =
          $.makeArray(document
          .getElementsByTagName("p"));
        array.reverse();
        $(array).appendTo(document.body);
      });
    </script>
  </head>

  <body>
    <h1>Creating an array</h1>
    <p>Now</p>
    <p>is</p>
    <p>the</p>
    <p>time</p>
  </body>
</html>
```

3. Add the code to get a list of <p> elements with getElementsById( ), convert the list into an array, reverse the array, and display the items in their resulting order (**Script 6.10**).

4. Save the file.

5. Navigate to the file, which creates a new array, reverses it, and shows the result (**Figure 6.5**). The list "Now" "is" "the" "time" reverses to "time" "the" "is" "Now."

Searching an Array

The jQuery array utility functions include the `$.inArray()` function, which lets you search an array for particular elements. Here's how you use this function:

`$.inArray(searchTerm, array))`

where *searchTerm* is the term you're searching for (for example, a string or a number), and *array* is the array you're searching. This function returns the 0-based index value in the array at which the first match on the search term was found, or –1 if the search term is not in the array.

To search an array:

1. Use a text editor (such as Microsoft WordPad) to create your Web page. We'll use the example inarray.html from the code for the book here.

2. Enter the code to add the jQuery library to the page and `<div>` elements to report on the results of searches (**Script 6.11**).

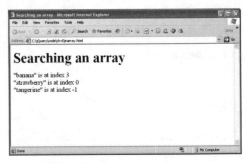

Figure 6.6 Searching an array.

Script 6.11 Adding <div> elements.

```
<html>
  <head>
    <title>Searching an array</title>
    <script
      src="http://code.jquery.com/jquery-
      latest.js">
    </script>
  </head>

  <body>
    <h1>Searching an array</h1>
    <div>"banana" is at index
      <span></span>
    </div>
    <div>"strawberry" is at index
      <span></span>
    </div>
    <div>"tangerine" is at index
      <span></span>
    </div>
  </body>
</html>
```

Script 6.12 Searching an array.

```
<html>
  <head>
    <title>Searching an array</title>
    <script
      src="http://code.jquery.com/jquery-
      latest.js">
    </script>

    <script>
    $(document).ready(function()
    {
      var array = ["strawberry",
        "vanilla", "chocolate",
        "banana"];

      $("span:eq(0)").text(
        $.inArray("banana", array));
      $("span:eq(1)").text(
        $.inArray("strawberry",
        array));
      $("span:eq(2)").text(
        $.inArray("tangerine", array));
    });
    </script>
  </head>

  <body>
    <h1>Searching an array</h1>
    <div>"banana" is at index
      <span></span>
    </div>
    <div>"strawberry" is at index
      <span></span>
    </div>
    <div>"tangerine" is at index
      <span></span>
    </div>
  </body>
</html>
```

3. Add the code to create an array and then search that array for various terms (**Script 6.12**).

4. Save the file.

5. Navigate to the file, which reports the results of various searches in the array, displaying the index value at which the search term was found (**Figure 6.6**).

Filtering an Array

One of the most powerful of the jQuery array utility functions is `$.grep()`, which lets you create new arrays by filtering existing ones.

Here's how you use `$.grep()` to, for example, create a new array of all elements in an existing array past index 4:

```
array = $.grep(array, function(n, i)
{
  return (i > 4);
});
```

Here's how you filter out all elements that contain 7:

```
array = $.grep(array, function (n)
{
  return n != 7;
});
```

To filter an array:

1. Use a text editor (such as Microsoft WordPad) to create your Web page. We'll use the example grep.html from the code for the book here.

2. Enter the code to add the jQuery library to the page and three `<div>` elements to display the results (**Script 6.13**).

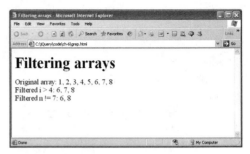

Figure 6.7 Filtering an array.

Script 6.13 Adding three `<div>` elements.

```
<html>
  <head>
    <title>Filtering arrays</title>
    <script
      src="http://code.jquery.com/jquery-
      latest.js">
    </script>
    <script>
      $(document).ready(function()
      {
        var array = [1, 2, 3, 4, 5, 6, 7, 8];
    </script>
  </head>
  <body>
    <h1>Filtering arrays</h1>
    <div id="div1"></div>
    <div id="div2"></div>
    <div id="div3"></div>
  </body>
</html>
```

Script 6.14 Filtering an array.

```
  Script
<html>
  <head>
    <title>Filtering arrays</title>
    <script
    src="http://code.jquery.com/jquery-
    latest.js">
    </script>
    <script>
      $(document).ready(function()
      {
        var array = [1, 2, 3, 4, 5, 6, 7, 8];
        $("#div1").text("Original array:
          " + array.join(", "));
        array = $.grep(array, function(n,
        i)
        {
          return (i > 4);
        });
        $("#div2").text("Filtered i > 4:
          " + array.join(", "));
        array = $.grep(array, function
        (n)
        {
          return n != 7;
        });
        $("#div3").text("Filtered n != 7:
           " + array.join(", "));
      });
    </script>
  </head>
  <body>
   <h1>Filtering arrays</h1>
    <div id="div1"></div>
    <div id="div2"></div>
    <div id="div3"></div>
  </body>
</html>
```

3. Add the code to filter the array, keeping only the elements past index 4 and filtering out those elements that equal 7 (**Script 6.14**).

4. Save the file.

5. Navigate to the file, which displays the array filtered in various ways (**Figure 6.7**).

Eliminating Duplicate Elements from Arrays

The jQuery function #.unique() removes duplicate elements from an array.

But there's a catch: $.unique() removes only duplicate elements that are page elements, not standard array elements such as strings and numbers. The reason for this limitation is that jQuery's mission is more to let you work with the elements in a page than to provide general utility functions that work on general arrays.

You use $.unique() when you have a set of page elements and want to weed out the duplicates before working with them.

We'll put $.unique() to work now with some <p> elements, some of which are duplicates.

To eliminate duplicate elements from an array:

1. Use a text editor (such as Microsoft WordPad) to create your Web page. We'll use the example unique.html from the code for the book here.

2. Enter the code to add the jQuery library to the page and some <p> elements, three of which have the class "duplicateMe" (**Script 6.15**).

Script 6.15 Adding new <p> elements.

```
<html>
  <head>
    <title>Eliminating duplicate
      elements</title>
    <script
      src="http://code.jquery.com/jquery-
      latest.js">
    </script>

  </head>
  <body>
    <h1>Eliminating duplicate elements</h1>
    <p class="duplicateMe"></p>
    <p class="duplicateMe"></p>
    <p class="duplicateMe"></p>
    <p></p>
  </body>
</html>
```

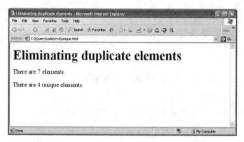

Figure 6.8 Determining the number of unique elements.

Script 6.16 Finding unique array page elements.

```
<html>
  <head>
    <title>Eliminating duplicate
      elements</title>
    <script
      src="http://code.jquery.com/jquery-
      latest.js">
    </script>

    <script>
      $(document).ready(function(){

        var array = $("p").get();

        array = array.concat(
          $(".duplicateMe").get());
        $("p:eq(1)").text("There are " +
          array.length + " elements.");

        array = jQuery.unique(array);
        $("p:eq(2)").text("There are " +
            array.length + " unique elements.");
      });
    </script>
  </head>
  <body>
    <h1>Eliminating duplicate elements</h1>
    <p class="duplicateMe"></p>
    <p class="duplicateMe"></p>
    <p class="duplicateMe"></p>
    <p></p>
  </body>
</html>
```

3. Add the code to put the <p> elements in an array, duplicate the three <p> elements with the class "duplicateMe" in the array, and then display the total number of elements and then the unique number of elements (**Script 6.16**).

4. Save the file.

5. Navigate to the file, which displays the total number of <p> elements in the array and then the number of unique <p> elements (**Figure 6.8**).

Checking Whether Data Is an Array

jQuery also has a utility function to determine whether an object is a true JavaScript array. This function, $.isArray(), returns a value of true if the object you pass it is an array, and false otherwise.

We'll put $.isArray() to work here in an example by creating an array and seeing whether $.isArray() can correctly determine that it is indeed an array.

To check whether data is an array:

1. Use a text editor (such as Microsoft WordPad) to create your Web page. We'll use the example is array.html from the code for the book here.

2. Enter the code to add the jQuery library to the page and create an array in code (**Script 6.17**).

Script 6.17 Creating an array.

```
<html>
  <head>
    <title>Testing for arrays</title>
    <script
      src="http://code.jquery.com/jquery-
      latest.js">
    </script>

    <script>
      $(document).ready(function(){
        var array = [1, 2, 3, 4, 5, 6, 7, 8];
      });
    </script>
  </head>

  <body>
    <h1>Testing for arrays</h1>
    <div></div>
  </body>
</html>
```

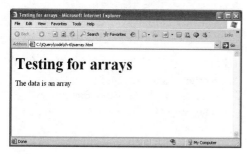

Figure 6.9 Checking for an array.

Script 6.18 Testing an array.

```
<html>
  <head>
    <title>Testing for arrays</title>
    <script
      src="http://code.jquery.com/jquery-
      latest.js">
    </script>

    <script>
      $(document).ready(function(){
        var array = [1, 2, 3, 4, 5, 6, 7, 8];
        if($.isArray(array)){
          $("div").text("The data is an
          array");
        }
        else {
          $("div").text("The data is not
          an array");
        }
      });
    </script>
  </head>

  <body>
    <h1>Testing for arrays</h1>
    <div></div>
  </body>
</html>
```

3. Add the code to check whether the array is indeed an array and then report the results of the test (**Script 6.18**).

4. Save the file.

5. Navigate to the file, which displays a message reporting that the array is indeed an array (**Figure 6.9**).

✔ Tip

■ You can also use the jQuery utility function #.isFunction( ) to check whether an object is a function.

Mapping an Array

A powerful array utility function that lets you save the steps of writing loops is `$.map()`, which lets you work with the individual elements in an array, modifying those elements and returning the new array. Mapping an array lets you translate every array element into something new.

Here's how you use `$.map()` to, for example, create a new array in which all elements are exactly double the value of the elements in the original array:

```
array = $.map(array, function(n, i)
{
  return (i + i);
});
```

Let's put this code to work.

To map an array:

1. Use a text editor (such as Microsoft WordPad) to create your Web page. We'll use the example map.html from the code for the book here.

2. Enter the code to add the jQuery library to the page, add two `<div>` elements to display the results, and create the array (**Script 6.19**).

Script 6.19 Creating an array in code.

```
<html>
  <head>
    <script
      src="http://code.jquery.com/jquery-
      latest.js">
    </script>

    <script>
      $(document).ready(function(){

        var array = [1, 2, 3, 4, 5];
      });
    </script>
  </head>

  <body>
    <h1>Mapping an array</h1>
    <div id="div1"></div>
    <div id="div2"></div>
  </body>
</html>
```

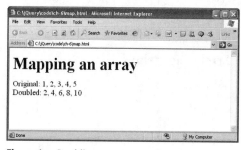

Figure 6.10 Doubling an array.

Script 6.20 Doubling an array's elements.

```
<html>
  <head>
    <script
      src="http://code.jquery.com/jquery-
      latest.js">
    </script>

    <script>
      $(document).ready(function(){

        var array = [1, 2, 3, 4, 5];
        $("#div1").text("Original: " +
          array.join(", "));

        array = $.map(array, function (i)
        {
          return i + i;
        });

        $("#div2").text("Doubled: " +
          array.join(", "));
      });
    </script>
  </head>

  <body>
    <h1>Mapping an array</h1>
    <div id="div1"></div>
    <div id="div2"></div>
  </body>
</html>
```

3. Add the code to map the array, doubling each element (**Script 6.20**).

4. Save the file.

5. Navigate to the file, which displays the original array and the doubled array (**Figure 6.10**).

MAPPING AN ARRAY

149

Trimming Text

The $.trim() function trims extra spaces from the front and end of text strings. This function is handy when you get text input from a user; you should always pass any text you read that the user has typed to $.trim() to clean up that text.

The example here displays a string of text that has leading and trailing spaces both before and after that string is passed to $.trim().

To trim text:

1. Use a text editor (such as Microsoft WordPad) to create your Web page. We'll use the example trim.html from the code for the book here.

2. Enter the code to add the jQuery library to the page, create the string with extra spaces in code, and add two <div> elements for displaying results (**Script 6.21**).

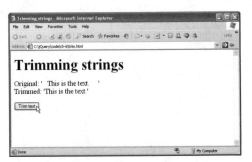

Figure 6.11 Trimming spaces from text.

Script 6.21 Creating a text string with extra spaces.

```
<html>
  <head>
    <title>Trimming strings</title>
    <script
      src="http://code.jquery.com/jquery-
      latest.js">
    </script>

    <script>
      $(document).ready(function(){
      var text =
      "   This is the text.    ";
       $("#target").text("Original: '" +
         text + "'");
      });
    });
    </script>
  </head>

  <body>
    <h1>Trimming strings</h1>
    <div id="target"></div>
    <div id="target2"></div>
  </body>
</html>
```

Script 6.22 Trimming text.

```
000                    Script
<html>
  <head>
    <title>Trimming strings</title>
    <script
      src="http://code.jquery.com/jquery-
      latest.js">
    </script>

    <script>
      $(document).ready(function(){
      var text =
      "   This is the text.      ";
       $("#target").text("Original: '" +
         text + "'");

      $("button").click(function ()
      {
        text = jQuery.trim(text);
        $("#target2").text("Trimmed: '" +
          text + "'");
      });

    });
    </script>
  </head>

  <body>
    <h1>Trimming strings</h1>
    <div id="target"></div>
    <div id="target2"></div>
    <form>
      <button>Trim text</button>
    </form>
  </body>
</html>
```

3. Add the code to trim the text (**Script 6.22**).

4. Save the file.

5. Navigate to the file, which displays the text with and without extra spaces (**Figure 6.11**).

JUMPING INTO AJAX

Ajax is a tool for creating rich, interactive Web applications—and with jQuery, you can easily implement it in your Web pages.

With Ajax, you can communicate with the server behind the scenes, with no page refresh—a cool feature because it makes Web-based applications seem just like desktop applications. That is, instead of the flash and flicker of pages being refreshed in your browser when the browser wants to get new data from the server, the browser quietly connects to the server and downloads the data it needs without a page refresh. And thanks to dynamic HTML, the browser can update page elements with the newly downloaded data also without a page refresh.

About Ajax

Thanks to Ajax, flickering pages in browsers are becoming a thing of the past in Web applications. Now you can make your selections in a Web page and see your results in the same page, with no page refresh needed, just as in a desktop application.

For example, you've probably seen those drop-down lists that appear beneath text fields as you start entering a search term; the code on the server tries to narrow down your search. With Ajax, JavaScript in the browser sends the partial search term as you're typing it to code on the server, which sends back guesses at what you're typing, which JavaScript displays in a clickable list box.

All of which is to say that JavaScript is essential to Ajax, because you need to execute a lot of code in the browser. That code has to read what the user wants to do, send that data to the server, read the response from the server, and display the interpreted data.

In fact, JavaScript is such an integral part of Ajax that it's part of the acronym "Ajax," which stands for Asynchronous JavaScript and XML.

What about the rest of the name? Ajax is asynchronous because it sends data to the server without making you wait for a response from the server—it just sets up a callback function that accepts whatever the server sends back, whenever it sends it back.

As for the XML part, when Ajax was originally developed, the data sent back from the server was usually in XML format, the lingua franca of data on the Web. You'd get a JavaScript XML object back from the server in your JavaScript—but such objects can be difficult to work with.

Although much Ajax still sends and receives data to and from the server in XML format, any text-based format works (it needs to be text based, because the HTTP that browsers use to communicate with servers is text based). In this chapter, we'll concentrate on how to read plain text data from the server, which is often preferable to dealing with data in XML format.

Coding Ajax yourself involves a lot of JavaScript. First, you have to create an XMLHttpRequest object, which is the foundation of Ajax work in browsers. Then you have to configure that object with any data you want to send to the server and set up and attach a callback function to the object to read the server's response. Next, you have to connect to the server with the object's send() function. Then you must interpret the response to make sure there was no error and extract the data sent to the browser from the XMLHttpRequest object.

Using jQuery, all this is as easy as pie. You just use a function like load(). That's all there is to it, as you will see.

✔ Tip

- You'll need to place the examples from this and the next chapter on a Web server to get them to work. Ajax is all about browsers communicating with servers using the XMLHttpRequest object, so you need to put these examples on a Web server and then browse to them in your browser (you can't just open the examples from disk).

Working with Ajax the Standard Way

We'll begin by putting Ajax to work the do-it-yourself way (without jQuery) to download a message from the server. The message will be in a file, message.txt, which contains the word "Hello." When the message is downloaded, it will be displayed. After seeing how to use Ajax the standard way, you'll see how to work with it the easy way—with jQuery—in the rest of the chapter.

To use Ajax the standard way:

1. Use a text editor (such as Microsoft WordPad) to create your Web page. We'll use the example ajax.html from the code for the book here.

2. Enter the code to create an XMLHttpRequest object and a `<div>` element to display the downloaded message (**Script 7.1**).

Script 7.1 Creating an XMLHttpRequest object.

```
<html>
  <head> <title>An Ajax example</title>
    <script language = "javascript">
      var XMLHttpRequestObject = false;
      if (window.XMLHttpRequest) {
        XMLHttpRequestObject = new
          XMLHttpRequest();
      } else if (window.ActiveXObject) {
        XMLHttpRequestObject = new
        ActiveXObject("Microsoft.XMLHTTP");
      }
    </script>
  </head>
  <body>
    <H1>An Ajax example</H1>
    <div id="targetDiv">
      <p>The fetched message will appear
        here.</p>
    </div>
  </body>
</html>
```

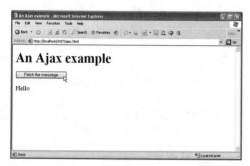

Figure 7.1 Displaying a fetched message.

Script 7.2 Connecting to the server.

```
<html>
  <head> <title>An Ajax example</title>
    <script language = "javascript">
      var XMLHttpRequestObject = false;
      if (window.XMLHttpRequest) {
        XMLHttpRequestObject = new
          XMLHttpRequest();
      } else if (window.ActiveXObject) {
        XMLHttpRequestObject = new
        ActiveXObject("Microsoft.XMLHTTP");
      }
      function getData(dataSource, divID){
        if(XMLHttpRequestObject) {
          var obj =
          document.getElementById(divID);
          XMLHttpRequestObject.open("GET",
            dataSource);
          XMLHttpRequestObject
          .onreadystatechange =
          function() {
            if (XMLHttpRequestObject
              .readyState == 4 &&
              XMLHttpRequestObject.status
              == 200) {
              obj.innerHTML =
                XMLHttpRequestObject
                .responseText; } }
```

3. Add the code to let the XMLHttpRequest object download message.txt from the server (**Script 7.2**).

4. Save ajax.html and message.txt on a Web server in the same directory.

5. Navigate to the file in your browser and click the button, which makes the page download message.txt and display the message (**Figure 7.1**).

Script 7.2 *continued*

```
          XMLHttpRequestObject
          .send(null);
          }
        }
    </script>
  </head>
  <body>
    <H1>An Ajax example</H1>
    <form>
      <input type = "button" value =
        "Fetch the message"
        onclick = "getData('message.txt',
          'targetDiv')">
    </form>
    <div id="targetDiv">
      <p>The fetched message will appear
        here.</p>
    </div>
  </body>
</html>
```

Using jQuery load( ) to Implement Ajax

jQuery has a number of functions that perform Ajax operations. One of the most popular is the load( ) function.

You use the load( ) function to display downloaded data in a wrapped set of elements (which, of course, can be only a single element, such as a <div> element) directly.

The load( ) function works like this:

load(*url*, *parameters*, *callback*)

Here, *url* is the URL of the resource you're fetching on the server, *parameters* is a JavaScript object whose properties hold values you want to send to the server, and *callback* is a callback function that jQuery will call when the Ajax operation is complete.

In this example, we'll use load( ) to download the file message.txt from the server behind the scenes when the page loads and display the contents of that file ("Hello") in a <div> element.

The URL here will be message.txt, so to get this example working, place message.txt in the same directory on the server as this example, load1.html. Of course, the URL can be of the form http://www.*domain/resource* as well.

One thing to know about Ajax: the URL you access must be in the same domain as the page itself, or the browser will display a warning dialog box. (To avoid this warning, you can use online code in the same directory as the page to access resources elsewhere on the Internet.)

Script 7.3 Creating a <div> element.

```
<html>
  <head>
    <title>Using the jQuery load()
      function</title>
    <script
      src="http://code.jquery.com/jquery-
      latest.js">
    </script>

  </head>

  <body>
    <h1>Using the jQuery load()
      function</h1>
    Got this from the server: <div></div>
  </body>
</html>
```

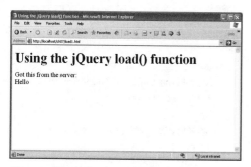

Figure 7.2 Displaying downloaded data.

Script 7.4 Accessing data on the server.

```
<html>
  <head>
    <title>Using the jQuery load()
      function</title>
    <script
      src="http://code.jquery.com/jquery-
      latest.js">
    </script>

    <script>
      $(document).ready(function(){
          $("div").load("message.txt");
      });
    </script>
  </head>

  <body>
    <h1>Using the jQuery load()
      function</h1>
    Got this from the server: <div></div>
  </body>
</html>
```

To use the jQuery load() function:

1. Use a text editor (such as Microsoft WordPad) to create your Web page. We'll use the example load1.html from the code for the book here.

2. Enter the code to add the jQuery library to the page and create a `<div>` element in which to display the contents of message. txt (**Script 7.3**).

3. Add the `load()` function, passing it the URL to access, `message.txt` (**Script 7.4**).

4. Save the load.html file and message.txt on a Web server in the same directory.

5. Navigate to the file in your browser, which makes the `load()` function download the text in message.txt (that is, "Hello") and display that text in the `<div>` element in the page (**Figure 7.2**).

Using Callbacks with the load( ) Function

The jQuery load( ) function works like this:

load(*url*, *parameters*, *callback*)

Here, *url* is the URL of the resource you're fetching on the server, *parameters* is a JavaScript object whose properties hold values you want to send to the server, and *callback* is a callback function that jQuery will call when the Ajax operation is complete.

You'll see how to use a callback function in this next example. When the Ajax operation is complete, the callback function, if you've specified one, is called.

In this example, we'll download message.txt, as in the previous two examples, and display a message in the page confirming that the Ajax download has been completed.

To use callbacks with load():

1. Use a text editor (such as Microsoft WordPad) to create your Web page. We'll use the example load2.html from the code for the book here.

2. Enter the code to add the jQuery library to the page and create a <div> element in which to display the contents of message. txt, as well as another <div> element in which to display the message from the callback function indicating that the download is complete (**Script 7.5**).

Script 7.5 Creating a target <div> element.

```
<html>
  <head>
    <title>Using the load() function with
    callbacks</title>
    <script
      src="http://code.jquery.com/jquery-
      latest.js">
    </script>

    <script>
      $(document).ready(function(){
        $("div").load("message.txt");
      });
    </script>
  </head>

  <body>
    <h1>Using the load() function with
    callbacks</h1>
    Got this from the server: <div></div>
    <div id="targetDiv"></div>
  </body>
</html>
```

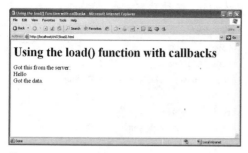

Figure 7.3 Using a callback function.

Script 7.6 Setting up a callback function.

```
<html>
  <head>
    <title>Using the load( ) functio
      callbacks</title>
    <script
      src="http://code.jquery.com/jquery-
      latest.js">
    </script>

    <script>
      $(document).ready(function(){
        $("div").load("message.txt",
          callback);
      });

      function callback()
      {
        $("#targetDiv").text("Got the
          data.");
      }
    </script>
  </head>

  <body>
    <h1>Using the load( ) function with
      callbacks</h1>
    Got this from the server: <div></div>
    <div id="targetDiv"></div>
  </body>
</html>
```

3. Add the load( ) function, passing it the URL to access, message.txt, and the name of the callback function (**Script 7.6**).

4. Save the load.html file and message.txt on a Web server in the same directory.

5. Navigate to the file in your browser, which makes the load( ) function download the text in message.txt (that is, "Hello") and display both that text and a message indicating that the download is complete in the <div> elements in the page (**Figure 7.3**).

Passing Data to the Server

The jQuery load( ) function lets you pass data to the server. Here's what load( ) looks like:

```
load(url, parameters, callback)
```

As before, *url* is the URL of the resource you're fetching on the server, *parameters* is a JavaScript object whose properties hold values you want to send to the server, and *callback* is a callback function that jQuery will call when the Ajax operation is complete.

If you include *parameters*, which is a JavaScript object with properties and values corresponding to the values you want to send to code on the server, load( ) sends that data using the POST method. If there is no parameters object, load( ) uses GET.

In this example, we'll post data to a PHP script on the server and display the message we get back (indicating whether we sent a 1 or a 2).

You'll need a PHP-enabled server for this example.

To pass data to the server:

1. Create the PHP script poster.php, which reads a parameter named data and sends a message indicating whether the data is a 1 or a 2 (**Script 7.7**).

2. In load3.html, enter the code to add the jQuery library to the page and create a <div> element to display the message from poster.php (**Script 7.8**).

Script 7.7 A sample PHP script.

```
<?php
if ($_POST["data"] == "1") {
echo 'You sent the server a value of 1';
}
if ($_POST["data"] == "2") {
echo 'You sent the server a value of 2';
}
?>
```

Script 7.8 Adding a <div> element.

```
<html>
  <head>
    <title>Using the jQuery load()
      function</title>
    <script
      src="http://code.jquery.com/jquery-
      latest.js">
    </script>

  </head>
  <body>
    <h1>Using the jQuery load()
      function</h1>
    Got this from the server: <div></div>
  </body>
</html>
```

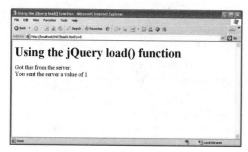

Figure 7.4 Passing data to the server.

Script 7.9 Sending data to the server.

```
● ● ●                Script
<html>
  <head>
    <title>Using the jQuery load()
      function</title>
    <script
      src="http://code.jquery.com/jquery-
      latest.js">
    </script>
    <script>
    $(document).ready(function(){
        $("div").load("poster.php",
        {data: 1});
    });
    </script>
  </head>
  <body>
    <h1>Using the jQuery load()
      function</h1>
    Got this from the server: <div></div>
  </body>
</html>
```

3. Add the load() function, passing it the URL to access, poster.php, and pass an object with the *data* property set to 1 (**Script 7.9**).

4. Save both files in the same directory on a PHP-enabled Web server.

5. Navigate to the file in your browser, which makes the load() function send the parameter named *data* with a value of 1 to poster.php and display the result in the <div> element in the page (**Figure 7.4**).

PASSING DATA TO THE SERVER

Passing Form Data to the Server

jQuery has a special function that makes it easy to pass the data from a form to the server using the load() function: the serializeArray() function.

This function, which takes no parameters, creates an object whose properties correspond to the names of the controls in a form, and whose property values are the values currently in the form controls. The serializeArray() function makes it easy to send a whole form's worth of data to the server.

In this example, we'll let the user enter a 1 or a 2 into a text field and then send that data to code on the server, which will return a matching message.

To pass form data to the server:

1. Create the PHP script poster.php to read a parameter named data and send a response indicating whether its value is a 1 or a 2 (**Script 7.10**).

2. In load4.html, enter the code to add the jQuery library to the page and create a <form> element with a text field named data as well as a button (**Script 7.11**).

Script 7.10 A PHP script that sends text.

```
<?php
if ($_POST["data"] == "1") {
echo 'You sent the server a value of 1';
}
if ($_POST["data"] == "2") {
echo 'You sent the server a value of 2';
}?>
```

Script 7.11 Creating a <form> element.

```
<html>
  <head>
    <title>Using the jQuery
    serializeArray() function</title>
    <script
    src="http://code.jquery.com/jquery-
    latest.js">
    </script>
  </head>
  <body>
    <h1>Using the jQuery serializeArray()
      function</h1>
    <form id="targetForm">
    Enter a 1 or 2:
    <input type="text" name="data"
      id="data"></input>
  <input type = "button" value="Check
    data" onclick="checker()"></input>
    </form>
    <br>
    Got this from the server: <div></div>
  </body>
</html>
```

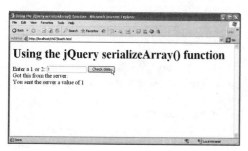

Figure 7.5 Passing form data.

Script 7.12 Sending form data to the server.

```
<html>
  <head>
    <title>Using the jQuery
    serializeArray() function</title>
    <script
    src="http://code.jquery.com/jquery-
    latest.js">
    </script>
      <script>
      function checker()
      {
      $("div").load("poster.php",
      $("#targetForm").serializeArray());
      }
      </script>
  </head>
  <body>
    <h1>Using the jQuery serializeArray()
      function</h1>
    <form id="targetForm">
    Enter a 1 or 2:
    <input type="text" name="data"
      id="data"></input>
   <input type = "button" value="Check
     data" onclick="checker()"></input>
    </form>
    <br>
    Got this from the server: <div></div>
  </body>
</html>
```

3. Now connect the button to a JavaScript function that calls load( ) to send the data in the text field to poster.php, which will send back a message, which appears in the <div> element (**Script 7.12**).

4. Save both files in the same directory on a PHP-enabled Web server.

5. Navigate to the file in your browser, enter 1 or 2 in the text field, and click the button to see the result from poster. php (**Figure 7.5**).

Using $.post( ) to Send Data to the Server

The load( ) function is handy for loading data from Ajax operations into a wrapped element set. It uses the GET method to communicate with the server, unless you pass data to the server, in which case it uses POST.

You may want more control over when the GET or POST method is used, and you may want to get your hands on the downloaded data without necessarily loading it into a wrapped element set automatically. For this, jQuery provides the $.get( ) and $.post( ) functions. These functions let you communicate with the server using the GET and POST methods, and they let you access the data without automatically loading it into a wrapped element set.

This example puts $.post( ) to work, sending data to the server and displaying the result. The arguments for $.post( ) are the same as for load( ).

To use $.post():

1. Create the PHP script poster.php to read a parameter named data and send a response indicating whether its value is a 1 or a 2 (**Script 7.13**).

2. In poster.html, enter the code to add the jQuery library to the page and create a <div> element to display the downloaded data (**Script 7.14**).

Script 7.13 A PHP script that sends text.

```php
<?php
if ($_POST["data"] == "1") {
echo 'You sent the server a value of 1';
}
if ($_POST["data"] == "2") {
echo 'You sent the server a value of 2';
}?>
```

Script 7.14 Creating a <div> display element.

```html
<html>
  <head>
    <title>Using the jQuery $.post()
      function</title>
    <script
      src="http://code.jquery.com/jquery-
      latest.js">
    </script>

  </head>

  <body>
    <h1>Using the jQuery $.post()
      function</h1>
    Got this from the server: <div></div>
  </body>
</html>
```

Figure 7.6 Passing data with $.post( ).

3. Add the code to make the page connect to the poster.php script when the page loads, sending it data and displaying the result in the <div> element (**Script 7.15**).

4. Save both files in the same directory on a PHP-enabled Web server.

5. Navigate to the file in your browser, which will send a value of 1 to the server and display the result (**Figure 7.6**).

Script 7.15 Sending data to the server with POST.

```
<html>
  <head>
    <title>Using the jQuery $.post()
      function</title>
    <script
      src="http://code.jquery.com/jquery-
      latest.js">
    </script>

    <script>
      $(document).ready(function(){
        $.post("poster.php", {data: 1},
        function(data){
          $("div").text(data);
        });
      });
    </script>
  </head>

  <body>
    <h1>Using the jQuery $.post()
      function</h1>
    Got this from the server: <div></div>
  </body>
</html>
```

Using the jQuery $.get( ) Function

You can use the $.get( ) function to get data from the server using the GET method. The $.get( ) function downloads the data you request from the server using the GET method and makes it available to a callback function.

The arguments for the $.get( ) function are the same as for the load( ) function.

This example uses the $.get( ) function to download the text in a file, message.txt, on the server and display that text. As earlier in this chapter, message.txt contains the text "Hello."

To use the jQuery $.get( ) function:

1. Use a text editor (such as Microsoft WordPad) to create your Web page. We'll use the example getter.html from the code for the book here.

2. Enter the code to add the jQuery library to the page and create a <div> element in which to display the contents of message. txt (**Script 7.16**).

Script 7.16 Creating a <div> element.

```
<html>
  <head>
    <title>Using the jQuery $.get()
      function</title>
    <script
      src="http://code.jquery.com/jquery-
      latest.js">
    </script>
  </head>

  <body>
    <h1>Using the jQuery $.get()
      function</h1>
    Got this from the server: <div></div>
  </body>
</html>
```

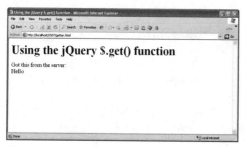

Figure 7.7 Displaying the downloaded data.

Script 7.17 Accessing the server with $.get().

```
<html>
  <head>
    <title>Using the jQuery $.get()
      function</title>
    <script
      src="http://code.jquery.com/jquery-
      latest.js">
    </script>

    <script>
      $(document).ready(function(){
      $.get("message.txt",
        function(data){
          $("div").text(data);
        });
      });
    </script>
  </head>

  <body>
    <h1>Using the jQuery $.get()
      function</h1>
    Got this from the server: <div></div>
  </body>
</html>
```

3. Add the $.get() function, passing it the URL to access, message.txt (**Script 7.17**).

4. Save the file on a Web server.

5. Navigate to the file in your browser, which makes the $.get() function download the text in message.txt (that is, "Hello") and display that text in the <div> element in the page (**Figure 7.7**).

Using $.get() to Send Data to the Server

The previous topic used the $.get() function to download data from the server in a static file using the GET method. You can also use the $.get() function to send data to the server.

✔ Tip

- The data you send to the server using the GET method is appended to the actual URL sent to the server, something like this: http://www.*server*.com/*pagename*?data=1. That means that, unlike with the POST method (which passes data in HTTP headers), your data will be visible to others. For more security when sending data to the server, use the POST method instead.

The arguments for the $.get() function are the same as for the load() function.

This example uses the $.get() function to send data to the server and get back a response, which the page then displays.

To use $.get() with data:

1. Create the PHP script getter.php to read a parameter named data and send a response indicating whether its value is a 1 or a 2 (**Script 7.18**).

2. In getter2.html, enter the code to add the jQuery library to the page and create a <div> element in which to display the results (**Script 7.19**).

Script 7.18 The getter.php script.

```
<?php
if ($_GET["data"] == "1") {
echo 'You sent the server a value of 1';
}
if ($_GET["data"] == "2") {
echo 'You sent the server a value of 2';
}?>
```

Script 7.19 Creating a <div> element for the results.

```
<html>
  <head>
    <title>Using the jQuery $.get()
      function with data</title>
    <script
      src="http://code.jquery.com/jquery-
      latest.js">
    </script>
  </head>

  <body>
    <h1>Using the jQuery $.get() function
      with data</h1>
    Got this from the server: <div></div>
  </body>
</html>
```

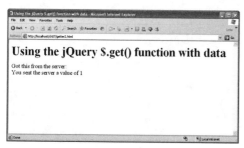

Figure 7.8 Passing data with $.get().

Script 7.20 Sending data to the server with $.get().

```
                    Script
<html>
  <head>
    <title>Using the jQuery $.get()
      function with data</title>
    <script
      src="http://code.jquery.com/jquery-
      latest.js">
    </script>

    <script>
      $(document).ready(function(){
        $.get("getter.php", {data: 1},
          function(data){
            $("div").text(data);
        });
      });
    </script>
  </head>

  <body>
    <h1>Using the jQuery $.get() function
      with data</h1>
    Got this from the server: <div></div>
  </body>
</html>
```

3. Add the code to use the $.get() function to send data to the server and then display the results you get back from the server (**Script 7.20**).

4. Save both files in the same directory on a PHP-enabled Web server.

5. Navigate to the file in your browser, which makes the page send data to getter.php on the server and display the result it gets back from the server (**Figure 7.8**).

171

USING THE FULL POWER OF AJAX

In the previous chapter, you saw a number of the Ajax functions available in jQuery: `load()`, `$.get()`, and so on. Those functions are good as quick Ajax solutions, but they're not complete solutions. What if you want to set a timeout period for your Ajax request? What if you want to take control of the `XMLHttpRequest` object creation process? What if you want to handle any errors returned by an operation?

For these tasks and more, jQuery provides the full-fledged `$.ajax()` function. This function gives you access to the full power of Ajax, while still staying in jQuery. This chapter is all about `$.ajax()`.

About $.ajax( )

You call $.ajax() with a pair of name and value options. jQuery provides 20 such options. For example, to set the type of request—GET or POST—you use the type option. To set the URL for the request, you use the url option. So to download message.txt from the server, you could use code like this:

```
<script>
  $(document).ready(function(){
    $.ajax({
      type: "GET",
      url: "message.txt"
    });
  });
</script>
```

How do you actually retrieve the data that came back from the server (which is the whole point of Ajax)? You can use the success option, which lets you set up a callback function that is called if the Ajax operation is successful. The callback function is passed the response from the server and a status code (this code is made up of the standard HTTP status code: for example, 200 means that the operation was successful).

Here's how you can display the text you downloaded using Ajax:

```
<script>
  $(document).ready(function(){
    $.ajax({
      type: "GET",
      url: "message.txt",
      success: callback
    });
  });

  function callback(data, status)
  {
    $("div").text(data);
  }
</script>
```

Table 8.1 lists all the options for the $.ajax() function.

✔ Tip

■ You'll need to place the examples from this chapter on a Web server and then browse to them in your browser (you can't just open the examples from disk).

Table 8.1

The $.ajax( ) Options

Option	Type	Does This
async	Boolean	Ajax requests are usually made asynchronously. If you need synchronous requests, set this option to false.
beforeSend	Function	This is a callback function in which you can modify the XMLHttpRequest object before it is used.
cache	Boolean	Setting this option to false forces the pages that you request to not be cached by the browser.
complete	Function	This callback function is called when the request finishes (after success and error callback functions are executed). The function gets passed two arguments: the XMLHttpRequest object and a string containing the type of success of the request.
contentType	String	This option sets the MIME type for the content of the request.
data	Object, String	This option contains data to be sent to the server. If the option is sent as an object, it has property and value pairs that correspond to the data you're sending to the server and their corresponding data values.
dataFilter	Function	This function handles the raw response data of the XMLHttpRequest object.
dataType	String	This option sets the type of data that you're expecting back from the server. If none is specified, jQuery will pass either responseXML or responseText to your success callback function. The available types are xml, html, script, json, jsonp, and text.
error	Function	This function is called if the request fails. The function is passed three arguments: the XMLHttpRequest object, a string describing the type of error, and an exception object.
fglobal	Boolean	Set this option to true to trigger global Ajax event handlers for this request.
ifModified	Boolean	This option lets the request be successful only if the response has changed since the last request.
jsonp	String	This option overrides the callback function name in a jsonp request.
password	String	This option sets the password used in response to an HTTP access authentication request.
processData	Boolean	When you want to send objects or other nonprocessed data, set this option to false.
scriptCharset	String	This option causes the request to be interpreted using a certain character set. It can be used only for requests with the jsonp or script data type and the GET type.
success	Function	This function is called if the request succeeds. The function is passed two arguments: the data returned from the server and a string describing the status.
timeout	Number	This option sets a timeout (in milliseconds) for the request.
type	String	This option sets the type of request to make (POST or GET). The default is GET.
url	String	This option sets the URL to request.
username	String	This option sets the username to be used in response to an HTTP access authentication request by the server.
xhr	Function	This callback function creates an XMLHttpRequest object. Override this function to create your own XMLHttpRequest object.

About $.ajax( )

Using $.ajax( ) to Download Text

This topic gets us started with the $.ajax( ) function.

In this example, we'll download and then display the contents of a file, message.txt. In this case, message.txt contains just the word "Hello," which will be displayed when the Ajax operation is complete—at which point, we'll make $.ajax( ) call a callback function indicating that the Ajax operation was successful.

✔ Tip

■ Be sure to upload message.txt and ajax-success.html to the same directory on your server.

To use the jQuery $.ajax( ) function:

1. Use a text editor (such as Microsoft WordPad) to create your Web page. We'll use the example ajaxsuccess.html from the code for the book here.

2. Enter the code to add the jQuery library to the page and create a <div> element to display the contents of message.txt in (**Script 8.1**).

Script 8.1 Creating a <div> element.

```
<html>
  <head>
    <title>Using the jQuery $.ajax()
      function</title>
    <script
      src="http://code.jquery.com/jquery-
      latest.js">
    </script>
  </head>

  <body>
    <h1>Using the jQuery $.ajax()
      function</h1>
    Got this from the server: <div></div>
  </body>
</html>
```

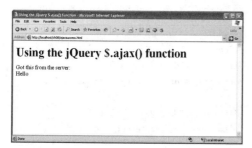

Figure 8.1 Displaying downloaded data.

Script 8.2 Accessing data on the server.

```
<html>
  <head>
    <title>Using the jQuery $.ajax()
      function</title>
    <script
      src="http://code.jquery.com/jquery-
      latest.js">
    </script>

    <script>
      $(document).ready(function(){
        $.ajax({
          type: "GET",
          url: "message.txt",
          success: callback
        });
      });

      function callback(data, status)
      {
        $("div").text(data);
      }
    </script>
  </head>

  <body>
    <h1>Using the jQuery $.ajax()
      function</h1>
    Got this from the server: <div></div>
  </body>
</html>
```

3. Add the `$.ajax()` function, passing it the URL to access, `"message.txt"`, the type of the request, `GET`, and a callback function that displays the downloaded text (**Script 8.2**).

4. Save the ajaxsuccess.html file and message.txt on a Web server in the same directory.

5. Navigate to the file in your browser, which makes the `$.ajax()` function download the text in message.txt (that is, "Hello") and display that text in the `<div>` element in the page (**Figure 8.1**).

Using $.ajax() to Post Data to the Server

jQuery allows the $.ajax() function to communicate with the server using the GET and POST methods, and it lets you access the data without automatically loading it into a wrapped element set.

This example puts $.ajax() to work sending data to the server using the POST method and displaying the result.

To post data using $.ajax():

1. Create the PHP script poster.php to read a parameter named "data" and send a response if its value is 1 or 2 (**Script 8.3**).

2. In ajaxpost.html, enter the code to add the jQuery library to the page and create a <div> element to display the downloaded data (**Script 8.4**).

Script 8.3 A PHP script that sends text.

```
<?php
if ($_POST["data"] == "1") {
echo 'You sent the server a value of 1';
}
if ($_POST["data"] == "2") {
echo 'You sent the server a value of 2';
}?>
```

Script 8.4 Creating a <div> display element.

```
<html>
  <head>
    <title>Using $.ajax() to post
      data</title>
    <script
      src="http://code.jquery.com/jquery-
      latest.js">
    </script>
    </script>
  </head>
  <body>
    <h1>Using $.ajax() to post data</h1>
    Got this from the server: <div></div>
  </body>
</html>
```

Figure 8.2 Posting data with $.ajax().

Script 8.5 Sending data to the server with POST.

```
<html>
  <head>
    <title>Using $.ajax() to post
      data</title>
    <script
      src="http://code.jquery.com/jquery-
      latest.js">
    </script>

    <script>
      $(document).ready(function(){
        $.ajax({
          type: "POST",
          url: "poster.php",
          data: {data: 1},
          success: callback
        });
      });
      function callback(data, status)
      {
        $("div").text(data);
      }
    </script>
  </head>
  <body>
    <h1>Using $.ajax() to post data</h1>
    Got this from the server: <div></div>
  </body>
</html>
```

3. Add the code to make the page connect to the poster.php script when the page loads, sending it data and displaying the result in the <div> element (**Script 8.5**).

4. Save both files in the same directory on a PHP-enabled Web server.

5. Navigate to the file in your browser, which will send a value of 1 to the server and display the result (**Figure 8.2**).

Using $.ajax( ) to Get Data from the Server

jQuery allows the $.ajax( ) function to communicate with the server using the GET and POST methods, and it lets you access the data without automatically loading it into a wrapped element set.

This example puts $.ajax( ) to work sending data to the server using the GET method and then displaying the result.

To use $.ajax( ) to get data:

1. Create the PHP script getter.php to read a parameter named "data" and send a response if its value is 1 or 2 (**Script 8.6**).

2. In poster.html, enter the code to add the jQuery library to the page and create a <div> element to display the downloaded data (**Script 8.7**).

Script 8.6 A PHP script that gets text.

```
<?php
if ($_GET["data"] == "1") {
echo 'You sent the server a value of 1';
}
if ($_GET["data"] == "2") {
echo 'You sent the server a value of 2';
}?>
```

Script 8.7 Creating a <div> element.

```
<html>
  <head>
    <title>Using $.ajax() to get
      data</title>
    <script
      src="http://code.jquery.com/jquery-
      latest.js">
    </script>
  </head>

  <body>
    <h1>Using $.ajax() to get data</h1>
    Got this from the server: <div></div>
  </body>
</html>
```

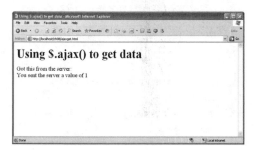

Figure 8.3 Getting data with $.ajax().

Script 8.8 Sending data to the server with GET.

```
                    Script
<html>
  <head>
    <title>Using $.ajax() to get
      data</title>
    <script
      src="http://code.jquery.com/jquery-
      latest.js">
    </script>

    <script>
      $(document).ready(function(){
        $.ajax({
          type: "GET",
          url: "getter.php",
          data: {data: 1},
          success: callback
        });
      });
      function callback(data, status)
      {
        $("div").text(data);
      }
    </script>
  </head>

  <body>
    <h1>Using $.ajax() to get data</h1>
    Got this from the server: <div></div>
  </body>
</html>
```

3. Add the code to make the page connect to the poster.php script when the page loads, sending it data with GET and displaying the result in the <div> element (**Script 8.8**).

4. Save both files in the same directory on a PHP-enabled Web server.

5. Navigate to the file in your browser, which will send a value of 1 to the server and display the result (**Figure 8.3**).

Handling Ajax Errors

Sometimes, things go wrong when you're working with Ajax. For example, the resource you're trying to download from the server may not be there, or there may be no connection to the Internet.

The `$.ajax()` function lets you handle errors with a callback function that's called when an error occurs. You connect the error callback function to the `$.ajax()` function using the `error` option and put error handling code into the callback function.

The error callback function is passed three items: the `XMLHttpRequest` object, a string that contains the error description, and an exception object.

In this example, we'll try to access a resource on the Web that isn't actually there and handle the error with code in an error handler.

To handle Ajax errors:

1. Use a text editor (such as Microsoft WordPad) to create your Web page. We'll use the example ajaxerror.html from the code for the book here.

2. Enter the code to add the jQuery library to the page and create a `<div>` element to display the results of the operation (**Script 8.9**).

Script 8.9 Creating a reporting <div> element.

```
<html>
  <head>
    <title>Handling Ajax errors</title>
    <script
      src="http://code.jquery.com/jquery-
      latest.js">
    </script>
  </head>

  <body>
    <h1>Handling Ajax errors</h1>
    Got this in response: <div></div>
  </body>
</html>
```

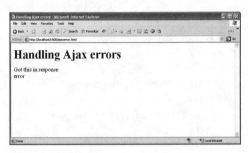

Figure 8.4 Displaying an error message.

Script 8.10 Handling an Ajax error.

```
<html>
  <head>
    <title>Handling Ajax errors</title>
    <script
      src="http://code.jquery.com/jquery-
      latest.js">
    </script>

    <script>
      $(document).ready(function(){
        $.ajax({
          type: "GET",
          url: "getterr.php",
          data: {data: 1},
          success: callback,
          error: err
        });
      });
        function callback(data, status)
        {
          $("div").text(data);
        }
        function err(xhr, reason, ex)
        {
          $("div").text(reason);
        }
    </script>
  </head>

  <body>
    <h1>Handling Ajax errors</h1>
    Got this in response: <div></div>
  </body>
</html>
```

3. Add the $.ajax() function, passing it a nonexistent URL to access, "getterr. php", the type of the request, GET, and an error callback function that displays the error string (**Script 8.10**).

4. Save the ajaxerror.html file on a Web server.

5. Navigate to the file in your browser, which makes the $.ajax() function attempt to connect to a nonexistent file on the server, returning the error message "error" (**Figure 8.4**).

Handling Ajax Timeouts

At times, you may not want to wait for an Ajax operation to complete if it's taking too long: for example, the resource you're trying to reach may not be available.

You can specify a timeout time in milliseconds with the `timeout` property of the `$.ajax()` function. This example does just that, timing out after 10 milliseconds.

To handle Ajax timeouts:

1. Use a text editor (such as Microsoft WordPad) to create your Web page. We'll use the example timeout.html from the code for the book here.

2. Enter the code to add the jQuery library to the page and create a `<div>` element in which to display the results of the Ajax operation (**Script 8.11**).

Script 8.11 Creating a new <div> element.

```
<html>
  <head>
    <title>Handling Ajax timeouts</title>
    <script
      src="http://code.jquery.com/jquery-
      latest.js">
    </script>
  </head>

  <body>
    <h1>Handling Ajax timeouts</h1>
    Got this in response: <div></div>
  </body>
</html>
```

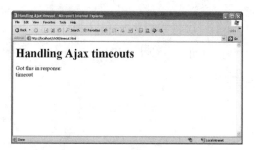

Figure 8.5 Displaying a timeout message.

Script 8.12 Handling an Ajax timeout.

```
<html>
  <head>
    <title>Handling Ajax timeouts</title>
    <script
      src="http://code.jquery.com/jquery-
      latest.js">
    </script>

    <script>
      $(document).ready(function(){
      $.ajax({
         type: "GET",
         url: "getter.php",
         data: {data: 1},
         success: callback,
         timeout: 10,
         error: err
       });
      });
      function callback(data, status)
      {
        $("div").text(data);
      }
      function err(xhr, reason, ex)
      {
        $("div").text(reason);
      }
    </script>
  </head>

  <body>
    <h1>Handling Ajax timeouts</h1>
    Got this in response: <div></div>
  </body>
</html>
```

3. Add the $.ajax() function, passing it the URL to access, "getter.php", the type of the request, GET, and the data to pass; then set the timeout property to 10 milliseconds and set the error callback function that displays the error string (**Script 8.12**).

4. Save the timeout.html and getter.php files in the same directory of a PHP-enabled Web server.

5. Navigate to timeout.html in your browser, which makes the $.ajax() function connect the server, but the whole operation times out almost immediately, returning the message "timeout" (**Figure 8.5**).

Handling XML

Ajax stands for Asynchronous JavaScript and XML, so let's now take a look at how to handle an XML document, sandwiches.xml, which lists several sandwich types:

```
<?xml version="1.0"?>
<sandwiches>
<sandwich>ham</sandwich>
<sandwich>turkey</sandwich>
<sandwich>cheese</sandwich>
</sandwiches>
```

You can specify the data type xml in the $.ajax() function to get back a JavaScript XML object, which you have to unravel by calling various functions. This example shows the sandwich types in a <select> control.

To handle XML:

1. Use a text editor (such as Microsoft WordPad) to create your Web page. We'll use the example ajaxxml.html from the code for the book here.

2. Enter the code to add the jQuery library to the page and create a <select> control to display the sandwiches (**Script 8.13**).

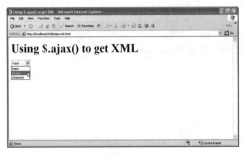

Figure 8.6 Displaying XML data.

Script 8.13 Creating a new <select> element.

```
<html>
  <head>
    <title>Using $.ajax() to get
    XML</title>
    <script
      src="http://code.jquery.com/jquery-
      latest.js">
    </script>
  </head>
  <body>
    <h1>Using $.ajax() to get XML</h1>
    <form>
      <select size="1" id="sandwichList">
        <option>Select a
          sandwich</option>
      </select>
    </form>
  </body>
</html>
```

Script 8.14 Handling XML in Ajax.

```
                    Script
<html>
  <head> ...
    </script>
    <script>
      $(document).ready(function(){
        $.ajax({
        type: "GET",
        url: "sandwiches.xml",
        dataType: "xml",
        success: callback
      });
      });
      function callback(data, status)
      {
        var sandwiches =
          data.getElementsByTagName(
            "sandwich");
          listSandwiches(sandwiches);
      }
      function listSandwiches
        (sandwiches)
      {
        var loopIndex;
        var selectControl =
          document.getElementById(
          'sandwichList');
        for (loopIndex = 0; loopIndex <
          sandwiches.length; loopIndex++)
        {
          selectControl.options[
          loopIndex] = new
            Option(sandwiches[loopIndex]
            .firstChild.data);
        }
      }
    </script>
  </head>
  <body>
    <h1>Using $.ajax() to get XML</h1>
    ...
  </body>
</html>
```

3. Add the `$.ajax()` function, setting `dataType` as `"xml"`, downloading sand-wiches.xml, and recovering the sandwich types from the JavaScript XML object returned (**Script 8.14**).

4. Save the ajaxxml.html and sandwiches. xml files in the same directory on a Web server.

5. Navigate to ajaxxml.html in your browser, which makes it download the sandwich types and display them in the `<select>` control (**Figure 8.6**).

Handling Ajax Events Globally

You can handle Ajax events such as a success or error event locally in the $.ajax() function, but jQuery also provides functions to connect a callback function to any of these events globally to handle all your Ajax operations (saving you the trouble of setting up local event handlers for each operation). These global event handlers are AjaxStart(), AjaxSend(), AjaxSuccess(), AjaxError(), AjaxComplete(), and AjaxStop(). This example puts global Ajax event handlers to work.

To handle Ajax events globally:

1. Use a text editor to create your Web page. We'll use the example globals.html from the code for the book here.

2. Enter the code to add the jQuery library to the page and create <div> elements to display the various events (**Script 8.15**).

Script 8.15 Creating new <div> elements.

```
<html>
  <head>
    <title>Handling Ajax events</title>
    <script
      src="http://code.jquery.com/jquery-
      latest.js">
    </script>
  </head>
  <body>
    <h1>Handling Ajax events</h1>
    <fiv id="starting">Starting...</div>
    <fiv id="sending">Sending...</div>
    <fiv id="success">Successful...</div>
    <fiv id="complete">Complete...</div>
    Got this in response: <div
      id="results"></div>
  </body>
</html>
```

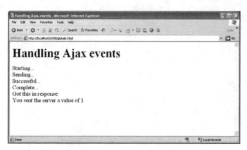

Figure 8.7 Displaying Ajax events.

3. Add the `$.ajax()` function and connect the global event handlers to display text when their events occur (**Script 8.16**).

4. Save globals.html and getter.php in the same directory in a PHP-enabled server.

5. Navigate to globals.html to track Ajax events as they happen (**Figure 8.7**).

Script 8.16 Handling Ajax global events.

```
Script
<html>
  <head>
    <title>Handling Ajax events</title>
    <script
    src="http://code.jquery.com/jquery-
    latest.js">
    </script>
    <script>
    $(document).ready(function(){
      $("#starting").hide();
      $("#sending").hide();
      $("#success").hide();
      $("#complete").hide();
      $("#starting").bind("ajaxStart",
        function(){
          $(this).show();
        });
      $("#sending").bind("ajaxSend",
        function(){
          $(this).show();
        });
      $("#success").bind("ajaxSuccess",
        function(){
          $(this).show();
        });
      ("#complete").bind("ajaxComplete",
        function(){
          $(this).show();
        });
```

Script 8.16 *continued*

```
Script
      $.ajax({
        type: "GET",
        url: "getter.php",
        data: {data: 1},
        success: callback
      });
    });
      function callback(data, status)
      {
        $("#results").text(data);
      }
    </script>
  </head>
  <body>
    <h1>Handling Ajax events</h1>
    <fiv id="starting">Starting...</div>
    <fiv id="sending">Sending...</div>
    <fiv id="success">Successful...</div>
    <fiv id="complete">Complete...</div>
    Got this in response: <div
      id="results"></div>
  </body>
</html>
```

USING THE JQUERY WIDGETS

This is a fun chapter. jQuery comes with a number of widgets, and we'll take a look them at here.

A widget is a control (controls are the text boxes, list boxes, buttons, and so on in a Web page) that augments what's available in standard HTML.

For example, one popular widget is the accordion, which lets you squeeze a lot of text into a small amount of space by displaying bars that, when clicked, open to more text.

Here are the jQuery widgets:

◆ Accordion

◆ Datepicker

◆ Dialog

◆ Progressbar

◆ Slider

◆ Tabs

About Working with Widgets

To put the widgets to work, we're going to have to include more prewritten JavaScript and stylesheets than we have before. In particular, we'll often need to include the CSS User Interface (UI) stylesheet, like this:

```
<link type="text/css" href=
 "http://jqueryui.com/latest/themes/
 base/ui.all.css" rel="stylesheet" />
```

And we'll often need the latest version of the jQuery library from jqueryui.com:

```
<script type="text/javascript"
 src="http://jqueryui.com/latest/
 jquery-1.3.2.js"></script>
```

We'll also need the ui.core.js library from jqueryui.com:

```
<script type="text/javascript"
 src="http://jqueryui.com/latest/ui/
 ui.core.js"></script>
```

And finally, we'll need the JavaScript code for the individual widgets themselves, such as ui.datepicker.js for the datepicker widget:

```
<script type="text/javascript"
 src="http://jqueryui.com/latest/ui/
 ui.datepicker.js">
</script>
```

OK, let's get to work and start creating some widgets!

Script 9.1 Adding the jQuery libraries.

```
<html>
  <head>
  <title>Using an accordion</title>
  <link type="text/css"
    href="http://jqueryui.com/latest/
    themes/base/ui.all.css"
    rel="stylesheet" />
  <script type="text/javascript"
    src="http://jqueryui.com/latest/
    jquery-1.3.2.js"></script>
  <script type="text/javascript"
    src="http://jqueryui.com/latest/
    ui/ui.core.js"></script>
  <script type="text/javascript"
    src="http://jqueryui.com/latest/ui/
    ui.accordion.js"></script>
  <script type="text/javascript">
  $(document).ready(function(){
    $("#accordion").accordion();
  });
  </script>
  </head>
  <body style="font-size:65%;">
  <h1>Using an accordion</h1>
  <div id="accordion">
  ...
  </div>
  </body>
</html>
```

Creating Accordion Widgets

Accordion widgets let you display content in the pleats of an accordion. When you click a pleat, it opens, showing you its content. This widget is particularly useful because screen space is always at a premium, and the accordion widget helps you make the most of it.

You organize the accordion's content into sections divided into <div> elements, and jQuery does the rest.

To create an accordion widget:

1. Use a text editor (such as Microsoft WordPad) to create your Web page. We'll use the example accordion.html from the code for the book here.

2. Enter the code to add the needed jQuery libraries to the page and create a <div> element to display the accordion widget (**Script 9.1**).

continues on next page

CREATING ACCORDION WIDGETS

3. Format the text for the accordion widget into <div> elements and create the accordion widget (**Script 9.2**).

Script 9.2 Creating an accordion widget.

```
○ ○ ○                    Script
<html>
  <head>
  <title>Using an accordion</title>
  ...
  <script type="text/javascript">
  $(document).ready(function(){
    $("#accordion").accordion();
  });
  </script>
  </head>
  <body style="font-size:65%;">
  <h1>Using an accordion</h1>
  <div id="accordion">
  <h3><a href="#">Section 1</a></h3>
  <div>
    <p>This is the first section.</p>
  </div>
  <h3><a href="#">Section 2</a></h3>
  <div>
    <p>This is the second section.  </p>
  </div>
  <h3><a href="#">Section 3</a></h3>
  <div>
    <p>This is the third section.</p>
    <ul>
      <li>List item one</li>
      <li>List item two</li>
      <li>List item three</li>
    </ul>
  </div>
  <h3><a href="#">Section 4</a></h3>
  <div>
    <p>This is the fourth section.</p>
  </div>
  </div>
  </body>
</html>
```

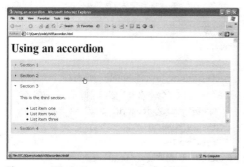

Figure 9.1 Displaying an accordion widget.

4. Save the file.

5. Navigate to the file in your browser, which makes the accordion widget appear; click a section pleat to display its interior content (**Figure 9.1**).

Creating Datepicker Widgets

Datepicker widgets display a clickable calendar control that lets users select dates.

You create a datepicker widget with the `datepicker()` function, connecting it to the `<div>` element in which you want the datepicker widget to appear.

You can read the date the user selected by creating an event handler for the onSelect event, whose handler is passed the data as a text string and an object corresponding to the datepicker widget:

```
$("#datepicker").datepicker({
onSelect: function(dateText, inst) {
  $("#result").text("You selected " +
    dateText)} });
```

To create a datepicker widget:

1. Use a text editor (such as Microsoft WordPad) to create your Web page. We'll use the example datepicker.html from the code for the book here.

2. Enter the code to add the needed jQuery libraries and create a `<div>` element to display the datepicker widget (**Script 9.3**).

Script 9.3 Creating a `<div>` element.

```
<html>
  <head>
  <title>Using a datepicker</title>
  <link type="text/css"
    href="http://jqueryui.com/latest/
    themes/base/ui.all.css"
    rel="stylesheet" />
  <script type="text/javascript"
    src="http://jqueryui.com/latest/
    jquery-1.3.2.js"></script>
  <script type="text/javascript"
    src="http://jqueryui.com/latest/
    ui/ui.core.js"></script>
  <script type="text/javascript"
    src="http://jqueryui.com/latest/ui/
    ui.accordion.js"></script>
  <script type="text/javascript">
$(document).ready(function(){
    $("#accordion").datepicker();
});
  </script>
  </head>
  <body style="font-size:65%;">
  <h1>Using a datepicker</h1>
  <div type="text" id="datepicker"></div>
  </body>
</html>
```

Script 9.4 Creating a datepicker widget.

```
<!DOCTYPE html>
<html>
<head>
  <title>Using a datepicker</title>
  <link type="text/css"
    href="http://jqueryui.com/latest/
    themes/base/ui.all.css"
    rel="stylesheet" />
  <script type="text/javascript"
    src="http://jqueryui.com/latest/
    jquery-1.3.2.js"></script>
  <script type="text/javascript"
    src="http://jqueryui.com/latest/
    ui/ui.core.js"></script>
  <script type="text/javascript"
    src="http://jqueryui.com/latest/ui/
    ui.accordion.js"></script>
  <script type="text/javascript">
  $(document).ready(function(){
    $("#accordion").datepicker();
  });
  </script>
  <script type="text/javascript">
  $(document).ready(function(){
    $("#datepicker").datepicker({
    onSelect: function(dateText, inst) {
      $("#result").text("You selected " +
        dateText)}
    });
  });
  </script>
  </head>
  <body style="font-size:65%;">
  <h1>Using a datepicker</h1>
  <div type="text" id="datepicker"></div>
  <div style="font-size:100%;"
  id="result"></div>
  </body>
</html>
```

3. Add the call to `datepicker()`, connecting an event handler to the onSelect event to display the selected date (**Script 9.4**).

continues on next page

4. Save the file.

5. Navigate to the file in your browser and click a date to see that date displayed; then pick another date and watch it appear on the screen (**Figure 9.2**).

Figure 9.2 Displaying a selected date.

Script 9.5 Creating a new <div> element.

```html
<html>
  <head>
  <title>Using a dialog</title>
  <link type="text/css"
  href="http://jqueryui.com/
  latest/themes/base/ui.all.css"
  rel="stylesheet" />
  <script type="text/javascript"
  src="http://jqueryui.com/
  latest/jquery-1.3.2.js"></script>
  <script type="text/javascript"
  src="http://jqueryui.com/
  latest/ui/ui.core.js"></script>
  <script type="text/javascript"
  src="http://jqueryui.com/
  latest/ui/ui.draggable.js"></script>
  <script type="text/javascript"
  src="http://jqueryui.com/
  latest/ui/ui.resizable.js"></script>
  <script type="text/javascript"
  src="http://jqueryui.com/
  latest/ui/ui.dialog.js"></script>
  </head>
  <body style="font-size:65%;">
  <h1>Using a dialog</h1>
  </body>
</html>
```

Creating Dialog Widgets

Dialog widgets are just what you expect them to be: dialog boxes. Using jQuery dialog widgets, you can create simple or elaborate dialog boxes with ease.

This example shows how to create a dialog widget with a button that closes it. The next example shows how to recover data that was entered in a dialog widget.

To create a dialog widget:

1. Use a text editor (such as Microsoft WordPad) to create your Web page. We'll use the example dialog.html from the code for the book here.

2. Enter the code to add the needed jQuery libraries and a <div> element to create the dialog widget (**Script 9.5**).

continues on next page

3. Add the code to create a dialog widget and the button to close it (**Script 9.6**).

Script 9.6 Creating a dialog widget.

```
<html>
  <head>
  <title>Using a dialog</title>
  <link type="text/css"
  href="http://jqueryui.com/
  latest/themes/base/ui.all.css"
  rel="stylesheet" />
  <script type="text/javascript"
  src="http://jqueryui.com/
  latest/jquery-1.3.2.js"></script>
  <script type="text/javascript"
  src="http://jqueryui.com/
  latest/ui/ui.core.js"></script>
  <script type="text/javascript"
  src="http://jqueryui.com/
  latest/ui/ui.draggable.js"></script>
  <script type="text/javascript"
  src="http://jqueryui.com/
  latest/ui/ui.resizable.js"></script>
  <script type="text/javascript"
  src="http://jqueryui.com/
  latest/ui/ui.dialog.js"></script>
  <script type="text/javascript">
  $(document).ready(function(){
    $("#dialog").dialog({
    buttons: {"Ok": function() {
      $(this).dialog("close"); } }
    });
  });
  </script>
  </head>
  <body style="font-size:65%;">
  <h1>Using a dialog</h1>
    <div id="dialog" title="Dialog
    Title">This is a dialog.
    </div>
  </body>
</html>
```

Figure 9.3 Displaying a dialog box.

4. Save the file.

5. Navigate to the file in your browser, which displays the dialog box (**Figure 9.3**). Click the Ok button to close the dialog box.

CREATING DIALOG WIDGETS

Getting Data from Dialog Widgets

You can also add controls to dialog widgets and read the data the user entered in them. This example displays a text field in a dialog widget and then displays whatever text that a user enters in it.

To get data from a dialog widget:

1. Use a text editor (such as Microsoft WordPad) to create your Web page. We'll use the example dialog2.html from the code for the book here.

2. Enter the code to add the needed jQuery libraries and create a <div> to display the dialog widget (**Script 9.7**).

Script 9.7 Creating a <div> element.

```
<html>
  <head>
  <link type="text/css"
  href="http://jqueryui.com/
  latest/themes/base/ui.all.css"
  rel="stylesheet" />
  <script type="text/javascript"
  src="http://jqueryui.com/
  latest/jquery-1.3.2.js"></script>
  <script type="text/javascript"
  src="http://jqueryui.com/
  latest/ui/ui.core.js"></script>
  <script type="text/javascript"
  src="http://jqueryui.com/
  latest/ui/ui.draggable.js"></script>
  <script type="text/javascript"
  src="http://jqueryui.com/
  latest/ui/ui.resizable.js"></script>
  <script type="text/javascript"
  src="http://jqueryui.com/
  latest/ui/ui.dialog.js"></script>
  </head>
  <body style="font-size:65%;">
  <h1>Getting data from a dialog</h1>
    <div id="dialog" title="Dialog
    Title">Enter some text and close me.
    <input type="text" id="text"></input>
    </div>
  </body></html>
```

Script 9.8 Reading text from a dialog widget.

```
<html>
  <head>
  <link type="text/css"
  href="http://jqueryui.com/
  latest/themes/base/ui.all.css"
  rel="stylesheet" />
  <script type="text/javascript"
  src="http://jqueryui.com/
  latest/jquery-1.3.2.js"></script>
  <script type="text/javascript"
  src="http://jqueryui.com/
  latest/ui/ui.core.js"></script>
  <script type="text/javascript"
  src="http://jqueryui.com/
  latest/ui/ui.draggable.js"></script>
  <script type="text/javascript"
  src="http://jqueryui.com/
  latest/ui/ui.resizable.js"></script>
  <script type="text/javascript"
  src="http://jqueryui.com/
  latest/ui/ui.dialog.js"></script>
  <script type="text/javascript">
  $(document).ready(function(){
  $("#dialog").dialog({
    buttons: {"Ok": function() {
    $(this).dialog("close"); } },
    beforeclose: function(event, ui) {
    $("#results").text("You entered " +
    $("#text").val())
   }
   });
  });
  </script>
  </head>
  <body style="font-size:65%;">
  <h1>Getting data from a dialog</h1>
    <div id="dialog" title="Dialog
    Title">Enter some text and close me.
    <input type="text" id="text"></input>
    </div>
    <div id="results"></div>
  </body></html>
```

3. Add the code to display the text field and read the text (**Script 9.8**).

4. Save the file.

continues on next page

5. Navigate to the file and enter text in the text field (**Figure 9.4**).

6. Click the Ok button to see the text the user entered (**Figure 9.5**).

Figure 9.4 Displaying a selected date.

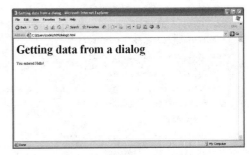

Figure 9.5 Displaying a selected date.

Script 9.9 Creating a <div> element.

```
<html><head>
  <title>Using a progress bar</title>
  <link type="text/css"
  href="http://jqueryui.com/
  latest/themes/base/ui.all.css"
  rel="stylesheet" />
  <script type="text/javascript"
  src="http://jqueryui.com/
  latest/jquery-1.3.2.js"></script>
  <script type="text/javascript"
  src="http://jqueryui.com/
  latest/ui/ui.core.js"></script>
  <script type="text/javascript"
  src="http://jqueryui.com/
  latest/ui/ui.draggable.js"></script>
  <script type="text/javascript"
  src="http://jqueryui.com/
  latest/ui/ui.resizable.js"></script>
  <script type="text/javascript"
  src="http://jqueryui.com/latest/ui
  /ui.progressbar.js"></script>
  <script type="text/javascript">
  $(document).ready(function(){
    $("#progressbar").progressbar({
      value: 30 });
    });
  </script>
</head>
<body style="font-size:65%;">
  <h1>Using a progress bar</h1>
  <div id="progressbar"></div>
</body></html>
```

Creating a Progressbar Widget

Progress bars are horizontal bars that indicate the progress of an operation. Here we'll display a progressbar widget that increases when a button is clicked.

To create a progressbar widget:

1. Use a text editor (such as Microsoft WordPad) to create your Web page. We'll use the example progressbar.html from the code for the book here.

2. Enter the code to add the needed jQuery libraries and create a <div> element to display the progressbar widget (**Script 9.9**).

continues on next page

3. Add a call to display the progressbar widget and increase the length of the bar when a button is clicked (**Script 9.10**).

4. Save the file.

Script 9.10 Creating a progressbar widget.

```
<html>
  <head>
  <title>Using a progress bar</title>
  <link type="text/css"
  href="http://jqueryui.com/
  latest/themes/base/ui.all.css"
  rel="stylesheet" />
  <script type="text/javascript"
  src="http://jqueryui.com/
  latest/jquery-1.3.2.js"></script>
  <script type="text/javascript"
  src="http://jqueryui.com/
  latest/ui/ui.core.js"></script>
  <script type="text/javascript"
  src="http://jqueryui.com/
  latest/ui/ui.draggable.js"></script>
  <script type="text/javascript"
  src="http://jqueryui.com/
  latest/ui/ui.resizable.js"></script>
  <script type="text/javascript"
  src="http://jqueryui.com/latest/ui
  /ui.progressbar.js"></script>
  <script type="text/javascript">
  $(document).ready(function(){
    $("#progressbar").progressbar({
      value: 30 });
    });
    function increase() {
    $("#progressbar")
      .progressbar('value', 80);
    }
  </script>
  </head>
  <body style="font-size:65%;">
    <h1>Using a progress bar</h1>
    <div id="progressbar"></div>
    <form>
    <input type="button" value="Increase"
      onclick="increase()"></input>
    </form>
  </body></html>
```

Figure 9.6 Displaying a progress bar.

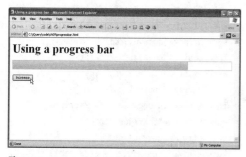

Figure 9.7 Increasing a progress bar.

5. Navigate to the file to see the progressbar widget (**Figure 9.6**).

6. Click the button to increase the length of the progress bar (**Figure 9.7**).

Creating a Slider Widget

Sliders are those horizontal sliding controls that look like they come from a stereo; jQuery supports them as well.

To create a slider widget:

1. Use a text editor (such as Microsoft WordPad) to create your Web page. We'll use the example slider.html from the code for the book here.

2. Enter the code to add the needed jQuery libraries and create a `<div>` element to display the slider widget (**Script 9.11**).

Script 9.11 Creating a `<div>` element.

```
<html>
  <head>
    <title>Using sliders</title>
    <link type="text/css"
    href="http://jqueryui.com/
    latest/themes/base/ui.all.css"
    rel="stylesheet" />
    <script type="text/javascript"
    src="http://jqueryui.com/
    latest/jquery-1.3.2.js"></script>
    <script type="text/javascript"
    src="http://jqueryui.com/
    latest/ui/ui.core.js"></script>
    <script type="text/javascript"
    src="http://jqueryui.com/
    latest/ui/ui.draggable.js"></script>
    <script type="text/javascript"
    src="http://jqueryui.com/
    latest/ui/ui.resizable.js"></script>
    <script type="text/javascript"
    src="http://jqueryui.com/latest/
    ui/ui.slider.js"></script>
    <style type="text/css">
      #slider { margin: 10px; }
    </style>
  </head>

  <body style="font-size:65%;">
    <h1>Using sliders</h1>
    <div id="slider"></div>
  </body>
</html>
```

Script 9.12 Creating a slider widget.

```
<html>
  <head>
  <title>Using sliders</title>
  <link type="text/css"
  href="http://jqueryui.com/
  latest/themes/base/ui.all.css"
  rel="stylesheet" />
  <script type="text/javascript"
  src="http://jqueryui.com/
  latest/jquery-1.3.2.js"></script>
  <script type="text/javascript"
  src="http://jqueryui.com/
  latest/ui/ui.core.js"></script>
  <script type="text/javascript"
  src="http://jqueryui.com/
  latest/ui/ui.draggable.js"></script>
  <script type="text/javascript"
  src="http://jqueryui.com/
  latest/ui/ui.resizable.js"></script>
  <script type="text/javascript"
  src="http://jqueryui.com/latest/
  ui/ui.slider.js"></script>
  <style type="text/css">
    #slider { margin: 10px; }
  </style>
  <script type="text/javascript">
  $(document).ready(function(){
    $("#slider").slider({min: 0, max:
      100,
      slide: function(event, ui) {
      $("#results").text("Slider is at "
      +$("#slider").slider('value'))}
    });
  });
  </script>
  </head>

  <body style="font-size:65%;">
    <h1>Using sliders</h1>
    <div id="slider"></div>
    <div id="results"></div>
  </body>
</html>
```

3. Add a call to display the slider widget and display the new value when the user slides the control (**Script 9.12**).

continues on next page

4. Save the file.

5. Navigate to the file to see the slider (**Figure 9.8**); slide the control to see the new value displayed.

Figure 9.8 Displaying a slider.

Script 9.13 Adding the jQuery libraries.

```
<html>
  <head>
    <title>Using tabs</title>
    <link type="text/css"
    href="http://jqueryui.com/
    latest/themes/base/ui.all.css"
    rel="stylesheet" />
    <script type="text/javascript"
    src="http://jqueryui.com/
    latest/jquery-1.3.2.js"></script>
    <script type="text/javascript"
    src="http://jqueryui.com/
    latest/ui/ui.core.js"></script>
    <script type="text/javascript"
    src="http://jqueryui.com/
    latest/ui/ui.draggable.js"></script>
    <script type="text/javascript"
    src="http://jqueryui.com/
    latest/ui/ui.resizable.js"></script>
    <script type="text/javascript"
    src="http://jqueryui.com/latest/
     ui/ui.tabs.js"></script>
  </head>
  <body style="font-size:65%;">
    <h1>Using tabs</h1>
  </body>
</html>
```

Creating a Tabs Widget

jQuery also lets you organize Web page content into tabs, and this example does exactly that.

To create a tabs widget:

1. Use a text editor (such as Microsoft WordPad) to create your Web page. We'll use the example tabs.html from the code for the book here.

2. Enter the code to add the needed jQuery libraries (**Script 9.13**).

continues on next page

3. Add the code to display the tabs widget and organize your data on the tabs (**Script 9.14**).

Script 9.14 Creating a tabs widget.

```html
<html>
  <head>
  <title>Using tabs</title>
  <link type="text/css"
  href="http://jqueryui.com/
  latest/themes/base/ui.all.css"
  rel="stylesheet" />
  <script type="text/javascript"
  src="http://jqueryui.com/
  latest/jquery-1.3.2.js"></script>
  <script type="text/javascript"
  src="http://jqueryui.com/
  latest/ui/ui.core.js"></script>
  <script type="text/javascript"
  src="http://jqueryui.com/
  latest/ui/ui.draggable.js"></script>
  <script type="text/javascript"
  src="http://jqueryui.com/
  latest/ui/ui.resizable.js"></script>
  <script type="text/javascript"
  src="http://jqueryui.com/latest/
   ui/ui.tabs.js"></script>
  <script type="text/javascript">
  $(document).ready(function(){
    $("#tabs").tabs();
  });
  </script>
  </head>
  <body style="font-size:65%;">
    <h1>Using tabs</h1>
  <div id="tabs">
    <ul>
      <li><a href="#fragment-
      1"><span>Item one</span></a></li>
      <li><a href="#fragment-
      2"><span>Item two</span></a></li>
      <li><a href="#fragment-
      3"><span>Item three</span></a></li>
    </ul>
    <div id="fragment-1">
        <p>This is tab one.</p></div>
    <div id="fragment-2">
        <p>This is tab two.</p></div>
    <div id="fragment-3">
        <p>This is tab three.</p></div>
    </div>
  </body>
</html>
```

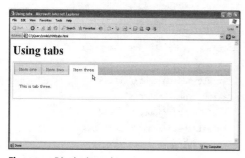

Figure 9.9 Displaying tabs.

4. Save the file.

5. Navigate to the file to see the tabs and click the tabs to see the page contents (**Figure 9.9**).

Adding Tabs to a Tabs Widget

You can also add new tabs to a tabs widget. This example does just that when the user clicks a button.

To add tabs to a tabs widget:

1. Use a text editor (such as Microsoft WordPad) to create your Web page. We'll use the example tabs2.html from the code for the book here.

2. Enter the code to add the needed jQuery libraries (**Script 9.15**).

Script 9.15 Adding the jQuery libraries.

```
<html>
  <head>
  <title>Adding tabs</title>
  <link type="text/css"
  href="http://jqueryui.com/
  latest/themes/base/ui.all.css"
  rel="stylesheet" />
  <script type="text/javascript"
  src="http://jqueryui.com/
  latest/jquery-1.3.2.js"></script>
  <script type="text/javascript"
  src="http://jqueryui.com/
  latest/ui/ui.core.js"></script>
  <script type="text/javascript"
  src="http://jqueryui.com/
  latest/ui/ui.draggable.js"></script>
  <script type="text/javascript"
  src="http://jqueryui.com/
  latest/ui/ui.resizable.js"></script>
  <script type="text/javascript"
  src="http://jqueryui.com/latest/
   ui/ui.tabs.js"></script>
  </head>
  <body style="font-size:65%;">
    <h1>Adding tabs</h1>
  </body>
</html>
```

Script 9.16 Adding new tabs.

```
<html>
  <head>
  <title>Adding tabs</title>
  <link type="text/css"
  href="http://jqueryui.com/
  latest/themes/base/ui.all.css"
  rel="stylesheet" />
  <script type="text/javascript"
  src="http://jqueryui.com/
  latest/jquery-1.3.2.js"></script>
  <script type="text/javascript"
  src="http://jqueryui.com/
  latest/ui/ui.core.js"></script>
  <script type="text/javascript"
  src="http://jqueryui.com/
  latest/ui/ui.draggable.js"></script>
  <script type="text/javascript"
  src="http://jqueryui.com/
  latest/ui/ui.resizable.js"></script>
  <script type="text/javascript"
  src="http://jqueryui.com/latest/
   ui/ui.tabs.js"></script>
  <script type="text/javascript">
  $(document).ready(function(){
    $("#tabs").tabs();
  });
  </script>
  </head>
  <body style="font-size:65%;">
    <h1>Adding tabs</h1>
  <div id="tabs">
    <ul>
      <li><a href="#fragment-
      1"><span>Item one</span></a></li>
      <li><a href="#fragment-
      2"><span>Item two</span></a></li>
      <li><a href="#fragment-
      3"><span>Item three</span></a></li>
    </ul>
    <div id="fragment-1">
        <p>This is tab one.</p></div>
    <div id="fragment-2">
        <p>This is tab two.</p></div>
    <div id="fragment-3">
        <p>This is tab three.</p></div>
    </div>
  </body>
</html>
```

3. Add the code to display the tabs widget and add a new tab when a button is clicked (**Script 9.16**).

continues on next page

4. Save the file.

5. Navigate to the file; you will see three tabs. Click the button to see a fourth tab added (**Figure 9.10**).

Figure 9.10 Adding a new tab.

INDEX

$( ) function, 6, 8, 12, 56
$.ajax( ) function, 173–189
   calling, 174
   downloading text with, 176–177
   getting data from server with, 180–181
   handling errors with, 182–183
   handling global events with, 188–189
   handling timeouts with, 184–185
   handling XML with, 186–187
   options for, 175
   posting data to server with, 178–179
   purpose of, 173, 174
$.browser variable, 128, 131–132
$.each( ) function, 128, 129–130
$.get( ) function, 166, 168–169, 170
$.grep( ) function, 142
$.inArray( ) function, 140
$.isArray( ) function, 128, 146
$.isFunction( ) function, 147
$.makeArray( ) function, 128, 138–139
$.map( ) function, 148
$.post( ) function, 166
$.support( ) function, 128, 135–136
$.trim( ) function, 150–151
$.unique( ) function, 128, 144
$.XXX( ) function, 127

A

accordion widget, 191, 193–195
addClass( ) function, 7
after( ) function, 74
Ajax, 153–189
   accessing full power of, 173
   and callback functions, 160–161
   coding, 155
   derivation of name, 154
   getting data from server, 168–169
   handling errors, 182–183
   handling global events, 188–189
   handling timeouts, 184–185
   handling XML document, 186–187
   jQuery support for, ix, 2
   overview, 154–155
   passing data to server, 162–167
   purpose of, ix, 153
   role of JavaScript in, 154
   using jQuery load( ) to implement,
     158–159
   using the standard way, 156–157
   and XML format, 154–155
AjaxComplete( ) event handler, 188
AjaxError( ) event handler, 188
AjaxSend( ) event handler, 188

`AjaxStart()` event handler, 188
`AjaxStop()` event handler, 188
`AjaxSuccess()` event handler, 188
`animate()` function, 104, 125–126
animation, 3, 103, 125–126
`append()` function, 54, 66–67, 68, 74
arrays, 138–149
  creating, 128, 138–139
  doubling, 149
  eliminating duplicate elements from,
    144–145
  filtering, 142–143
  functions for working with, 128
  getting unique members of, 128, 144–145
  identifying, 128, 146–147
  mapping, 148–149
  searching, 140–141
Asynchronous JavaScript and XML, 2, 154,
  186. *See also* Ajax
`attr()` function, 58–59, 60–61
`[attribute]` selector, 28, 40–41
attributes
  matching elements with specific, 28–29
  reading, 58–59
  setting values for, 60–61
  using nonstandard, 61
`[attribute=value]` selector, 29, 42–43

B

`before()` function, 74
`beforeunload()` function, 86
`bind()` function, 82, 84, 86
binding
  click events, 101
  event handlers, 82–83
  hover events, 99
  keyUp events, 97
  multiple event handlers, 84–85
  using shortcuts, 86–87
`blur()` function, 86
box model, W3C CSS, 135, 137
`boxModel` value, 135, 137

browsers
  checking available features in, 128,
    135–136
  customizing HTML for, 133–137
  determining type/version, 128, 131–132
  and drag-and-drop operations, 80
  and event handling, 79
  flickering pages in, 154
  and JavaScript, 1, 2
  and jQuery, 2
  and jQuery functions, 54
  tailoring HTML to specific, 128
buttons, 29, 48–49, 191

C

calendar control, 196
callback functions
  and animations, 125
  and fading operation, 113, 115, 123
  setting up, 161
  and show/hide operations, 104, 107
  and slide operation, 117, 119, 121
  and toggle operation, 111
  using with `load()` function, 160–161
calling event handlers, 88–89
capital letters, 97
capturing
  hover events, 99–100
  keystrokes, 97–98
Cascading Style Sheets, 2. *See also* CSS
`change()` function, 86
check boxes, 48–49
`checked` selector, 48
child elements
  selecting first/last, 34–35
  selecting *n*th, 36–37
`click()` function, 86–87
click events
  binding, 83, 86, 101
  connecting to event handlers, 90
  vs. double-clicks, 95
  triggering, 83
  unbinding, 90–91

`clicker()` function, 91, 95
`clone()` function, 54
code, running, 12–13
code files, xi
collections, 138
`contains(text)` selector, 38–39
controls, 191
coordinates, getting mouse event, 93–94
CSS
    box model, 135, 137
    meaning of acronym, 2
    selectors, 27
    styles, 10
    User Interface (UI) stylesheet, 192
    width/height properties, 55
`css()` function, 14, 54, 56
`cssFloat` value, 135

D

data
    getting from dialog widget, 202–204
    sending to server
        with `$.get()` function, 170–171
        with `load()` function, 162–165
        with `$.post()` function, 166-167
        with `POST`, 166–167
database, initializing, 88
`datepicker()` function, 196, 197
datepicker widget, 191, 192, 196–198
`dblclick()` function, 86
descendants, selecting direct, 32–33
dialog boxes, 199
dialog widget, 191, 199–204
direct descendants, selecting, 32–33
`<div>` elements
    animating expansion of, 126
    converting to `<span>` elements, 62–63
    putting wrapped sets into, 72
    selecting `<p>` elements descended from, 32
    wrapping `<p>` elements inside, 54
downloading text, 176–177
drag-and-drop operations, 80

duration
    for custom animations, 125
    for fading elements in/out, 113, 115
    for partially fading elements, 123
    showing/hiding elements with, 107–108
    for sliding elements up/down, 117, 119
    toggling element visibility with, 111–112
    for toggling sliding operations, 121
dynamic HTML, 63, 153

E

`each()` function, 54
`each` loop, 128
easing function, 125
effects, 103–126
    animating elements, 125–126
    fading elements in/out, 113–116
    jQuery support for, 3, 103
    overview, 104
    partially fading elements, 123–124
    showing/hiding elements, 17, 105–108
    sliding elements up/down, 22–23, 117–120
    toggling element visibility, 109–112
    toggling sliding operations, 121–122
elements
    animating, 125–126
    appending content to, 66–67
    appending other elements to, 74
    checking type of matched, 44–45
    cloning, 54
    counting number of, 8, 9
    displaying number of, 9
    fading in/out, 104, 113–116
    fading partially, 123–124
    gradually hiding, 104
    in hierarchies, 20–21
    inserting, 74–75
    looping over, 56–57
    moving, 67, 68–69
    replacing text in, 64–65
    returning width/height of, 55
    rewriting HTML for, 62–63

elements *(continued)*
    selecting
        by attribute, 40–41
        by attribute value, 42–43
        by ID, 6–7
        by position, 46–47
        by style, 10–11
    selecting first set of, 14–15
    selecting one of a set of, 18–19
    selecting set of, 8–9
    selecting user-selected, 50–51
    setting width/height of, 70–71
    showing/hiding, 16–17, 105–108
    sliding up/down, 22–23, 117–120
    toggling sliding operation for, 121–122
    toggling visibility of, 109–112
    wrapping, 54, 72–73
eq selector, 28, 46, 47
error( ) function, 86
error handling, Ajax, 182–183, 188
even selector, 28, 37
event handlers
    binding multiple, 84–85
    binding to events, 82–83
    calling, 88–89
    global, 188–189
    purpose of, 80
    unbinding, 90–91
event handling, 79, 80–81
event object methods, 92
event object properties, 80, 92
event targets, 101–102
event types, 95–96
events, 79–102
    binding event handlers to, 82–87
    capturing hover, 99–100
    determining type of, 95–96
    purpose of, 79
    unbinding, 90–91
    and Web browsers, 79
examining
    checked boxes/radio buttons, 48–49
    user-selected elements, 50–51

F

fadeIn( ) function, 115–116, 123
fadeOut( ) function, 113–114, 123
fades, 104, 113–116, 123–124
fadeTo( ) function, 123
filtering arrays, 142–143
Firefox, 80, 137. *See also* Web browsers
first-child selector, 29, 34–35
first selector, 14–15
focus( ) function, 86
form data, passing to server, 164–165
form elements, setting value of, 55, 76
functions, 53–77
    for appending content to elements, 66–67
    callback. *See* callback functions
    for checking whether objects are
        functions, 147
    for editing value attribute, 76–77
    examples of, 54–55
    for inserting elements, 74–75
    for looping elements in wrapped set, 56–57
    vs. methods, 53
    for moving page elements, 68–69
    by name
        $( ), 6, 8, 12, 56
        $.ajax( ), 173–189
        $.each( ), 128, 129–130
        $.get( ), 166, 168–169, 170
        $.grep( ), 142
        $.inArray( ), 140
        $.isArray( ), 128, 146
        $.isFunction( ), 147
        $.makeArray( ), 128, 138–139
        $.map( ), 148
        $.post( ), 166
        $.support( ), 128, 135–136
        $.trim( ), 150–151
        $.unique( ), 128, 144
        $.XXX( ), 127
        addClass( ), 7
        after( ), 74

animate(), 104, 125–126
append(), 54, 66–67, 68, 74
attr(), 58–61
before(), 74
beforeunload(), 86
bind(), 82, 84, 86
blur(), 86
change(), 86
click(), 86–87
clicker(), 91, 95
clone(), 54
css(), 14, 54, 56
datepicker(), 196, 197
dblclick(), 86
each(), 54
error(), 86
fadeIn(), 115–116, 123
fadeOut(), 113–114, 123
fadeTo(), 123
focus(), 86
getElementsById(), 27, 138, 139
height(), 55, 70–71
hide(), 16–17, 104, 105–106
hover(), 99
html(), 54, 62–63
innerText(), 54
insertAfter(), 24–25, 54
insertBefore(), 25
is(), 44–45
jquery(), 6, 8
jquery.XXX(), 127
keydown(), 86
keypress(), 86
keyup(), 86
load(), 86, 158–161
mousedown(), 86
mouseenter(), 86
mouseleave(), 86
mousemove(), 86
mouseout(), 86
mouseover(), 86

mouseup(), 86
one(), 88
out(), 99
outerHTML(), 54
over(), 99
resize(), 86
scroll(), 86
select(), 86
send(), 155
serializeArray(), 164
show(), 16–17, 104, 105–106
size(), 9
slice(), 58
slideDown(), 22–23
slideToggle(), 104, 121
slideUp(), 22–23, 117–118
submit(), 86
text(), 54, 64–65
toggle(), 104, 109–112
toggleClass(), 7
unbind(), 90
unload(), 86
val(), 55, 76
width(), 55, 70–71
wrap(), 54, 72–73
purpose of, 53
for reading attribute values, 58–59
for rewriting elements' HTML, 62–63
for rewriting elements' text, 64–65
for setting attribute values, 60–61
for setting element width/height, 70–71
utility. *See* utility functions
and Web browsers, 54
for wrapping elements, 72–73

G

GET method, 162, 166, 170, 180–181
getElementsById() function, 27, 138, 139
global event handlers, 188–189
gt selector, 47

H

headers, toggling visibility of, 109–112
`height()` function, 55, 70–71
`hide()` function, 16–17, 104, 105–106
hierarchies, selector, 20–21
`hover()` function, 99
hover events, capturing, 99–100
`hrefNormalized` value, 135
HTML
    creating, 24–25
    customizing by browser type, 133–137
    directly accessing, 54
    dynamic, 63, 153
    how jQuery handles, 3
    inserting, 24–25
    rewriting elements', 62–63
`html()` function, 54, 62–63
`htmlSerialize` value, 135
HTTP, 155, 170, 174, 175

I

ID value
    recovering/displaying, 101–102
    selecting elements by, 6–7, 27
image elements. *See* `<img>` elements
`<img>` elements
    binding click events for, 101
    fading in/out, 113–116
    getting/displaying ID value of, 101–102
    looping, 56–57
    setting width/height of, 70–71
    showing/hiding, 105–108
    triggering click event for, 83
index value, 18–19, 29, 36
initialization process, 88
`innerHTML` function, 54
`innerHTML` property, 18–19
`innerText()` function, 54
`insertAfter()` function, 24–25, 54
`insertBefore()` function, 25
interactive Web applications, 153

Internet Explorer, 80, 133. *See also* Web
    browsers
`is()` function, 44–45
italicizing text, 33, 34, 99–100

J

JavaScript
    and Ajax, 154
    arrays, 138
    cross-browser issues, 1, 2
    event handling in, 79, 80–81
    `getElementsById()` function, 27, 138, 139
    vs. jQuery utility functions, 127
    learning to use, xi
    libraries, ix, 1
    making pages come alive with, 79
    and Web 2.0, 1
    and widgets, 192
jQuery
    and Ajax, ix. *See also* Ajax
    animation support, 3, 103
    code files, xi
    creator of, 1
    cross-browser support, 2
    downloading, 4–5
    event handling in, 79, 80–81. *See also*
        events
    features, 2–3
    functions, 53–55. *See also* functions
    getting started with, 4–5
    how page loads are handled by, 3
    and HTML, 3
    installing, 4–5
    JavaScript library. *See* jQuery library
    methods, 53
    official Web site, 4
    popularity of, ix, x
    purpose of, ix, x, 1
    selector language, 2
    selectors, 30–31. *See also* selectors
    utility functions. *See* utility functions

visual effects, x, 3, 103. *See also* visual effects

widgets, x, 191. *See also* widgets

jquery( ) function, 6, 8

jQuery library
and Ajax widgets, 192
file extension for, 4
installing in any Web page, 5
minimized *vs.* full version, 4

jquery.com, 4

jqueryui.com, 192

jquery.XXX( ) function, 127

.js extension, 4

K

keyCode property, 97

keydown( ) function, 86

keyDown events, 97

keypress( ) function, 86

keyPress events, 97

keystrokes, capturing, 97–98

keyup( ) function, 86

keyUp events, 97

L

language attribute, 40–41

last-child selector, 29, 34–35

last selector, 15

leadingWhitespace value, 135

list boxes, 50, 191

listeners, 80. *See also* event handlers

load( ) function
and event handlers, 86
implementing Ajax with, 158–159
passing data to server with, 162–163
using callbacks with, 160–161

looping
<img> elements, 56–57
over object members, 128, 129–130

lt selector, 47

M

<marquee> element, 133–134

matched elements, checking type of, 44–45

methods, 53, 92

Microsoft WordPad, 6

mouse events, getting coordinates for, 93–94

mouse hover events, 99–100

mousedown( ) function, 86

mouseenter( ) function, 86

mouseleave( ) function, 86

mousemove( ) function, 86

mouseout( ) function, 86

mouseover( ) function, 86

mouseup( ) function, 86

moving page elements, 67, 68–69

N

noCloneEvent value, 135

nth-child(n) selector, 29, 36–37

O

object members
displaying, 130
looping over, 128, 129–130

object properties, 80

objectAll value, 135

objects, creating, 129

odd selector, 28, 37

one( ) function, 88

online database, initializing, 88

onload events, 3, 12

opacity value, 135

out( ) function, 99

outerHTML( ) function, 54

over( ) function, 99

P

\<p\> elements
  counting, 8
  creating, 24–25
  displaying number of, 9
  inserting, 24–25, 74–75
  italicizing, 33, 34
  selecting
    by ID, 6–7
    by index value, 18–19
    by style, 10–11
  selecting set of, 8–9
  showing/hiding, 16–17
  sliding, 22–23
  sliding up/down, 117–120
  styling, 10, 12
  wrapping inside \<div\> elements, 54
page elements
  animating, 125–126
  appending content to, 66–67
  appending other elements to, 74
  checking type of matched, 44–45
  cloning, 54
  counting number of, 8, 9
  displaying number of, 9
  fading in/out, 104, 113–116
  fading partially, 123–124
  gradually hiding, 104
  in hierarchies, 20–21
  inserting, 74–75
  looping over, 56–57
  moving, 67, 68–69
  replacing text in, 64–65
  returning width/height of, 55
  rewriting HTML for, 62–63
  selecting
    by attribute, 40–41
    by attribute value, 42–43
    by ID, 6–7
    by position, 46–47
    by style, 10–11

    selecting first set of, 14–15
    selecting one of a set of, 18–19
    selecting set of, 8–9
    selecting user-selected, 50–51
    setting width/height of, 70–71
    showing/hiding, 16–17, 105–108
    sliding up/down, 22–23, 117–120
    toggling sliding operation for, 121–122
    toggling visibility of, 109–112
    wrapping, 54, 72–73
page refresh, 2, 153, 154
pageX property, 92, 93–94
pageY property, 92, 93–94
paragraph elements
  counting, 8
  creating, 24–25
  displaying number of, 9
  inserting, 24–25, 74–75
  italicizing, 33, 34
  selecting
    by ID, 6–7
    by index value, 18–19
    by style, 10–11
  selecting set of, 8–9
  showing/hiding, 16–17
  sliding, 22–23
  sliding up/down, 117–120
  styling, 10, 12
  wrapping inside \<div\> elements, 54
PHP, Ajax examples and, xi
PHP script
  posting data to, 162–163
  for reading data, 164, 170, 178, 180
  for sending data to server, 166
positional selectors, 14, 46–47
POST method, 162, 166, 178
progress bars, 205
progressbar widget, 191, 205–207
properties
  event object, 80, 92
  mouse event, 93
  width/height, 55

R

radio buttons, 29, 48–49
`radio` selector, 29
Resig, John, 1
`resize()` function, 86
Rochester Institute of Technology, 1
running code, 12–13

S

`screenX` property, 93–94
`screenY` property, 93–94
`<script>` element, 5
`scriptEval` value, 135
`scroll()` function, 86
searching arrays, 140–141
`select()` function, 86
`<select>` control, 50, 186
`selected` selector, 29, 50
selecting. *See also* selectors
    checked check boxes, 48–49
    direct descendants, 32–33
    elements
        by attribute, 40–41
        by attribute value, 42–43
        by ID, 6–7
        by position, 46–47
        with specific text, 38–39
        by style, 10–11
    even/odd elements, 28, 37
    first child element, 29, 34–35
    first set of elements, 14–15
    last child element, 29, 34–35
    last set of elements, 14
    *n*th-child element, 29, 36–37
    one of a set of elements, 18–19
    selected radio buttons, 29, 48
    set of page elements, 8–9
    by specifying elements in hierarchy, 20–21
    user-selected elements, 50–51
selector hierarchies, 20
selector language, jQuery, 2

selectors. *See also* selecting
    creating chains of, 10
    examples of, 28–29
    passing to `jquery()` function, 8
    positional, 14, 46–47
    purpose of, 8, 27
    table of, 30–31
`send()` function, 155
`serializeArray()` function, 164
server
    accessing data on, 159, 168–169
    connecting to, 157
    downloading message from, 156–157
    getting data from, 180–181
    passing form data to, 164–165
    sending data to
        with `$.get()` function, 170–171
        with `load()` function, 162–163
        with `$.post()` function, 166–167
        with `POST` method, 178–179
`shiftKey` property, 97
shortcuts, binding event handlers using, 86–87
`show()` function, 16–17, 104, 105–106
`size()` function, 9
`slice()` function, 58
`slideDown()` function, 22–23
slider widget, 191, 208–210
sliders, 208
`slideToggle()` function, 104, 121
`slideUp()` function, 22–23, 117–118
sliding page elements, 22–23
spaces, trimming from text, 150–151
`<span>` elements, 62, 63
`String.fromCharCode()` method, 97
`style` value, 135
styles, selecting elements based on, 10–11
stylesheets, 192
`submit()` function, 86
success events, 188
`success` option, 174

T

tabs widget, 191, 211–216
target property, 92, 100, 101
tbody value, 135
text
    downloading, 176–177
    italicizing, 33, 34, 99–100
    replacing elements', 64–65
    selecting elements with specific, 38–39
    trimming spaces from, 150–151
text() function, 54, 64–65
text boxes, 191
text editor, 6
text fields, form, 76–77
timeout property, 184–185
toggle() function, 104, 109–112
toggleClass() function, 7
transitions, 104, 107
trimming text, 150–151
type option, 174
type property, 95

U

UI stylesheet, CSS, 192
uicore.js library, 192
ui.datapicker.js, 192
unbind() function, 90
unload() function, 86
url option, 174
User Interface (UI) stylesheet, CSS, 192
utility functions, 127–151
    for checking browser support for specific
        features, 135–136
    for creating arrays, 138–139
    for customizing HTML by browser type,
        133–137
    for determining browser type, 131–132
    for eliminating duplicate elements from
        arrays, 144–145
    examples of, 128
    for filtering arrays, 142–143
    for identifying arrays, 146–147

    vs. JavaScript, 127
    for looping over object members, 129–130
    for mapping arrays, 148–149
    purpose of, x, 127. See also functions
    for searching arrays, 140–141
    for trimming text, 150–151

V

val() function, 55, 76
value attribute, 76–77
values
    reading attribute, 58–59
    setting attribute, 60–61
visibility, toggling element, 109–110
visual effects, 103–126
    animating elements, 125–126
    fading elements in/out, 113–116
    jQuery support for, 3, 103
    overview, 104
    partially fading elements, 123–124
    showing/hiding elements, 17, 105–108
    sliding elements up/down, 22–23, 117–120
    toggling element visibility, 109–112
    toggling sliding operations, 121–122

W

W3C box model, 135, 137
Web 2.0, 1
Web-based applications, 153
Web browsers
    checking available features in, 128,
        135–136
    customizing HTML for, 133–137
    determining type/version, 128, 131–132
    and drag-and-drop operations, 80
    and event handling, 79
    flickering pages in, 154
    and JavaScript, 1, 2
    and jQuery, 2
    and jQuery functions, 54
    tailoring HTML to specific, 128

Web pages
    changing structure of, 54
    inserting elements in, 74–75
    inserting HTML in, 24–25
    installing jQuery library in, 5
    moving elements around in, 68–69, 74–75
    responding to user actions on, 79. *See also* events
    running code for, 12–13
    setting width/height of elements in, 70–71
Web server
    accessing data on, 159, 168–169
    connecting to, 157
    downloading message from, 156–157
    getting data from, 180–181
    passing form data to, 164–165
    sending data to
        with `$.get()` function, 170–171
        with `load()` function, 162–163
        with `$.post()` function, 166–167
        with `POST` method, 178–179
widgets, 191–216
    creating specific
        accordion, 193–195
        datepicker, 196–198
        dialog, 199–204
        progressbar, 205–207

        slider, 208–210
        tabs, 211–216
    and CSS User Interface stylesheet, 192
    and JavaScript, 192
    and jQuery library, 192
    purpose of, x, 191
    working with, 192
`width()` function, 55, 70–71
WordPad, 6
`wrap()` function, 54, 72–73
wrapped sets
    getting elements from, 58
    looping over elements in, 56–57
    purpose of, x
    putting into `<div>` elements, 72

X

x > y selector, 28
x selector, 28
X/Y coordinates, 93
x y selector, 28
XML format, 154–155, 186–187
`XMLHttpRequest` object, 155, 156–157, 182

Z

Zip file, xi

GET UP AND RUNNING QUICKLY!

For more than 15 years, the practical approach to the best-selling *Visual QuickStart Guide* series from Peachpit Press has helped millions of readers—from developers to designers to system administrators and more—get up to speed on all sorts of computer programs. Now with select titles in full color, *Visual QuickStart Guide* books provide an even easier and more enjoyable way for readers to learn about new technology through task-based instruction, friendly prose, and visual explanations.

Task-Based
Information is broken down into concise, one- and two-page tasks to help you get right to work.

Visual
Hundreds of screen shots illustrate the steps and show you the best way to do them.

Step by Step
Numbered, easy-to-follow instructions guide you through each task.

Tips
Lots of helpful tips are featured throughout the book.

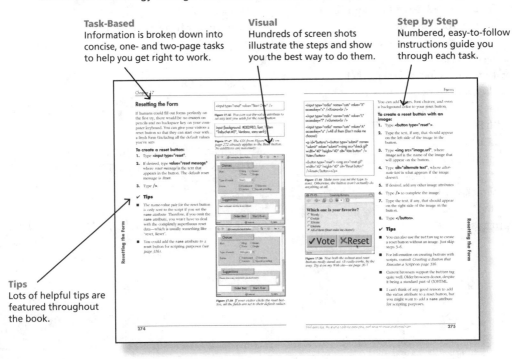

MICROSOFT **WINDOWS VISTA** SECOND EDITION
Learn Windows Vista the Quick and Easy Way!
CHRIS FEHILY

PHOTOSHOP CS4
Learn Photoshop the Quick and Easy Way!
ELAINE WEINMANN
PETER LOUREKAS

JAVASCRIPT & AJAX SEVENTH EDITION
Learn JavaScript and Ajax the Quick and Easy Way!
TOM NEGRINO
DORI SMITH

PHOTOSHOP ELEMENTS 7
Learn Photoshop Elements the Quick and Easy Way!
JEFF CARLSON

DREAMWEAVER CS4
Learn Dreamweaver CS4 the Quick and Easy Way!
TOM NEGRINO
DORI SMITH